You Can Sing!

Jerald B. Stone

Amsco Publications
New York/London/Sydney

Acknowledgements

Thanks to Wayne Adams and Dennis Anderson, whose encouragement stimulated the writing of the original manuscript.

Thanks also to Peter Pickow, whose advice in developing the final manuscript was invaluable.

To Amy Appleby,
whose faith and trust in me made this book possible.

Order No. AM 76175
US International Standard Book Number: 0.8256.2579.3
UK International Standard Book Number: 0.7119.1902.X

Exclusive Distributors:
Music Sales Corporation
257 Park Avenue South, New York, NY 10010, USA
Music Sales Limited
8/9 Frith Street, London W1V 5TZ, England
Music Sales Pty. Limited
120 Rothschild Street, Rosebery, Sydney, NSW 2018, Australia

Printed in the United States of America by
Vicks Lithograph and Printing Corporation

Table of Contents

Introduction

Your voice is a unique musical instrument—a wonderful expression of your feelings and personality. This book will help you discover your voice and gain technical knowledge—as you take a step-by-step adventure through the exciting world of vocal music. This proven method is designed to provide basic vocal training for singers of all levels—and has brought amazing results to thousands of beginners and professionals seeking to bring out the best in their vocal performance.

The first section of this book is a vocal coaching session. In this section, you will sing several songs in different styles and learn the techniques professional pop, rock, and Broadway singers use to add power to their vocal performance and increase their range. Exercises are provided during the coaching session to help you strengthen your new-found skills. You'll even learn how to create your own exercises to correct problems that may occur in new songs.

A complete voice lesson is provided in the second section of this book. This covers the finer points of singing and includes exercises for a daily vocal warmup that will free and strengthen your voice. This kind of daily program is used by most professional singers—and is highly recommended for students who wish to realize their vocal talents. This voice lesson actually contains enough information for many lessons—and can be used over a period of time to develop your voice. For students interested in a professional career, this program can be a perfect supplement to a voice class or private vocal instruction.

The human voice is the most remarkable of all instruments because it can be changed at will. You will have hours of fun learning to sing songs in many different styles with many different kinds of sounds. Complete arrangements of these songs are provided at the end of the book. If you are a singer who also plays piano or guitar, you can practice accompanying yourself. Or, if you have a friend who plays one of these instruments, you can enjoy performing together. (It's important for you to get performance experience—so don't turn down opportunities to perform for others.)

Go at your own pace when using this book. There is enough information contained here to provide you with a broad, ongoing program of vocal study for years to come. In fact, you will find many occasions during your singing career to repeat these voice-building exercises—or to get some professional tips on a particular vocal technique or style. Many students also find that the songs included in the vocal coaching session make excellent pieces for auditions and performances.

As you probably know, with a little study and practice, anyone can sing. In fact, your commitment to an ongoing program of vocal study will not only bring out the best in your vocal instrument—it can pave the way for a professional singing career.

Vocal Coaching Session

This coaching session is designed to allow you to apply your natural talents to the performance of top vocal hits. These are provided in the section "Song Arrangements" at the back of the book. As you work on each of these songs, you will find out how to perfect your sense of pitch, vocal placement, and tone quality. You will also learn how to get across the lyrics of a song—and how to make your performance truly meaningful. Exercises are provided along the way to help you practice everything from pronunciation and breathing to song phrasing and stylistic embellishments. For the male vocalist, there's a special section on rock-style falsetto singing—while female singers are coached on how to belt out a song. You will also get to devote special attention to identifying and developing your individual vocal range—and learn how to select music and adapt it to your personal performance needs.

Let's begin the session by looking at the lyrics of a song—and find out how the lyricist and singer use emotional meanings to add drama to a song's story.

Lyrics

Songs contain both music and lyrics. Although the music portion of a song may be recorded or played as an instrumental piece, technically speaking, a song is not a song without the *lyrics.* The term "lyrics" is especially appropriate because the words of songs are lyrical—that is, they are selected for their poetry and ability to convey feelings of emotion. Lyrics usually feature rhyme—and the individual rhymes in a song lyric often provide important guidelines for its general pronunciation.

As you become familiar with the lyrics of a song, you should also be aware of any emotional qualities or deeper meanings in the words. Let's take a close look at "Here's That Rainy Day," a versatile song that has been recorded by many famous pop and jazz performers—among them, Frank Sinatra, Andy Williams, Dinah Shore, Dionne Warwick, Ella Fitzgerald, and Stevie Wonder. Read the lyrics to "Here's That Rainy Day," and become familiar with the story they tell.

> Maybe I should have saved those leftover dreams;
> Funny, but here's that rainy day.
>
> Here's that rainy day they told me about,
> And I laughed at the thought that it might turn out this way.
>
> Where is that worn-out wish that I threw aside;
> After it brought my lover near?
>
> Funny how love becomes a cold rainy day.
> Funny that rainy day is here.

These lyrics have emotional meaning that is expressed from a personal point of view. They also use ***metaphor*** to involve the listener's imagination. A metaphorical expression describes one thing as though it were another. A lyric which uses metaphors is known as a *connotative lyric.* This kind of lyric implies something more than the exact meaning of the words. Here, a "cold, rainy day" is a metaphor for the end of a love affair.

Always be aware of the emotional meanings expressed in song lyrics. As you perform a song, tell the story of the lyrics from a sincere and personal point of view. This is the only sure way to involve an audience in your performance—and to stimulate their imaginations.

Pitch

Your *musical ear*—that is, your ability to hear musical ideas—is probably more important to singing than any part of your voice. Your ear makes it possible to copy sounds and memorize them—and enables you to sing melodies with or without accompaniment. In popular (or non-classical) styles of singing, the melody is seldom played in the accompaniment. This places added responsibility on the singer's ear.

All great singers have an excellent sense of pitch, which simply means that they have developed their ability to accurately hear musical notes. The term *pitch* refers to the number of vibrations per second assigned to a certain note. For example, orchestras tune to the A note above Middle C. This A note vibrates at 440 cycles per second. If you have *perfect pitch* (sometimes called *absolute pitch*), you can sing this A note without the aid of a piano or other instrument. Very few people have this ability, but most singers can develop a very good sense of pitch through study and practice.

Now turn to the section "Song Arrangements" and take a look at the song, "Here's That Rainy Day." If you are already familiar with this classic pop tune, you should have no trouble singing through it. If you play an instrument, you can play each note of the melody as you sing it to be sure that you are singing on pitch. Close listening to a good recording of a standard version of any song can also help you become familiar with its melody. Or, you can work together with a friend who plays an instrument to learn this piece. In any case, sing through "Here's That Rainy Day" until you are familiar with the melody.

Pop Placement

It is always a good idea to warm up your voice at the beginning of each vocal practice session, or before a performance. The exercises that follow will help you do this. They will also teach you to focus your voice in the placement used by many popular artists.

The first exercise will warm up your voice as you sing the vowel sound "oo" (as in the word "food"). Form the "oo" sound with your lips, then sing this five-tone scale exercise. As you vocalize this sound, you should feel its vibrations in the front of your mouth near your lips. If you are singing the "oo" correctly, you can pinch your nostrils while singing and the tone will not be interrupted.

Now, sing the same scale exercise on "oo" followed by a hummed "m." The hum should sound beautiful and full. You should feel the hum in your nose near your nostrils. To check if you are humming correctly, pinch your nostrils as you hum and the humming will stop. If you are humming incorrectly, the hum will continue when you hold your nostrils closed. If this is the case, just try it again. Both the "oo" and the hum should feel easy and relaxed to you as you sing them.

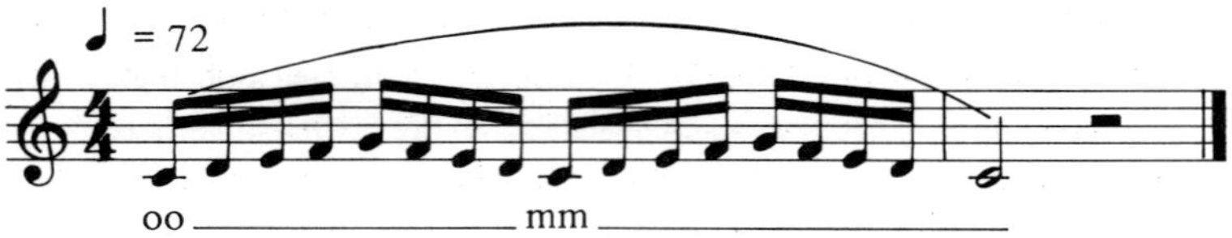

Now, turn back to the arrangement of "Here's That Rainy Day" and practice singing the melody on "oo" all the way through the song. Repeat the song, humming the "m" sound all the way through. This is good practice for sustaining a smooth vocal line in any song.

Range

The term *range* simply refers to the span of notes a particular voice or instrument is able to produce. This term may also be used to describe the span of notes required by a particular song.

Before you can select music to perform, you need to know your vocal range. Many singers with naturally low voices can sing very high, and many relatively high voices may also go quite low. The span of notes that you can sing with ease determines your vocal range. The span of notes you can sing most comfortably is technically called *tessitura.*

Vocal ranges are naturally grouped into five-note sections. Most singers have a comfortable range of about ten notes. Trained singers may have a comfortable range of fifteen notes or more. Sing each five-note section in this example to determine which is most comfortable. Use your normal voice when singing these notes. Select the five-note span that is most comfortable (your tessitura) and the adjacent five notes that are also comfortable. The label that includes these two sections names your vocal range.

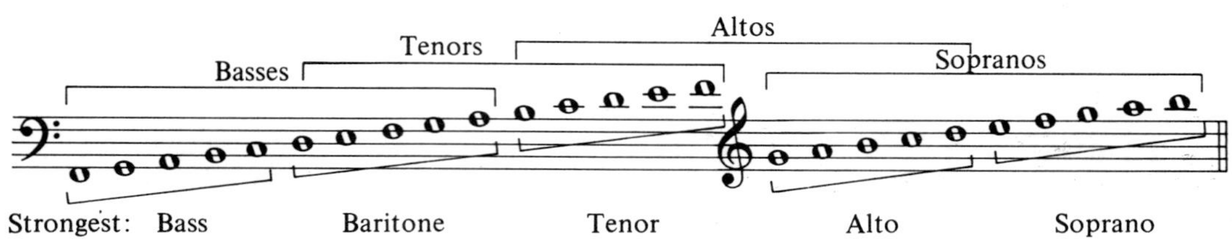

When you select music, look at the notes and be sure they fall within your ten-note range. If not, the song will have to be transposed or rearranged (see the sections "Selecting Music" and "Transposing" for a further discussion).

Your vocal range may determine your vocal quality. Altos and basses usually have deep or dark voices. Sopranos and tenors usually have bright or light voices. If your range and quality match, great. If they don't, you may find your range changing with practice. However, sometimes range and quality remain separate. In opera, dramatic tenors and sopranos have high voices that are also deep. Lyric baritones often have low voices that are contrastingly light. Do not be concerned with these labels. Go by your feeling of comfort when singing—and be sure to sing music that is within your range.

When writing about notes and note ranges, musicians often use this system of note names.

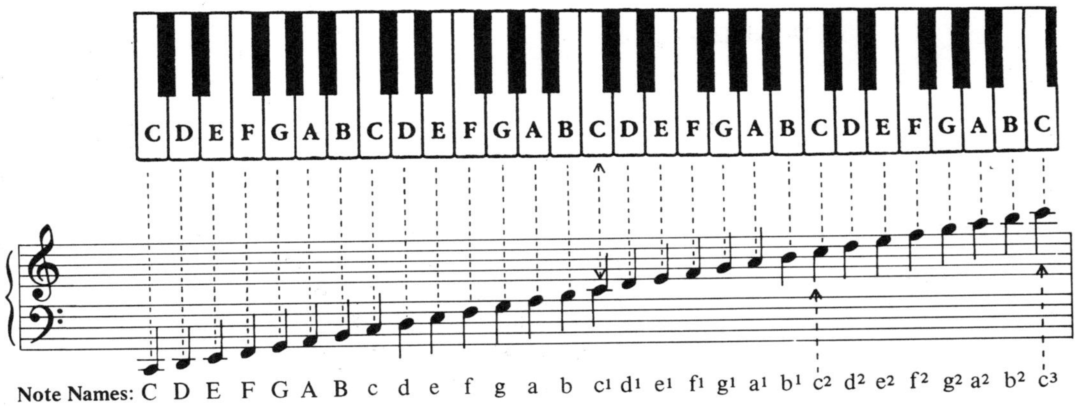

This system makes it possible to indicate an exact pitch without actually showing the note on a musical *staff.*

The Middle Register

Most pop singers use the ***middle register*** of the voice almost exclusively. In classical singing, tones in this register are often referred to as *mouth tones.* Many female singers today call this register "the mix." That is because the middle register lies between the ***chest register*** of the low voice and the ***head register*** of the high voice—and is produced by mixing the two resonances, head and chest.

The middle register is sometimes also called the *middle voice.* In the chart that follows, the middle voice is divided into the *lower-middle voice* (from c1 to g1) and the *upper-middle voice* (from a1 to e2). This includes most of the notes in "Here's That Rainy Day." Most people can sing in this range. (Note that male voices sound one octave lower than the melody line as written.)

Register and Resonance Chart

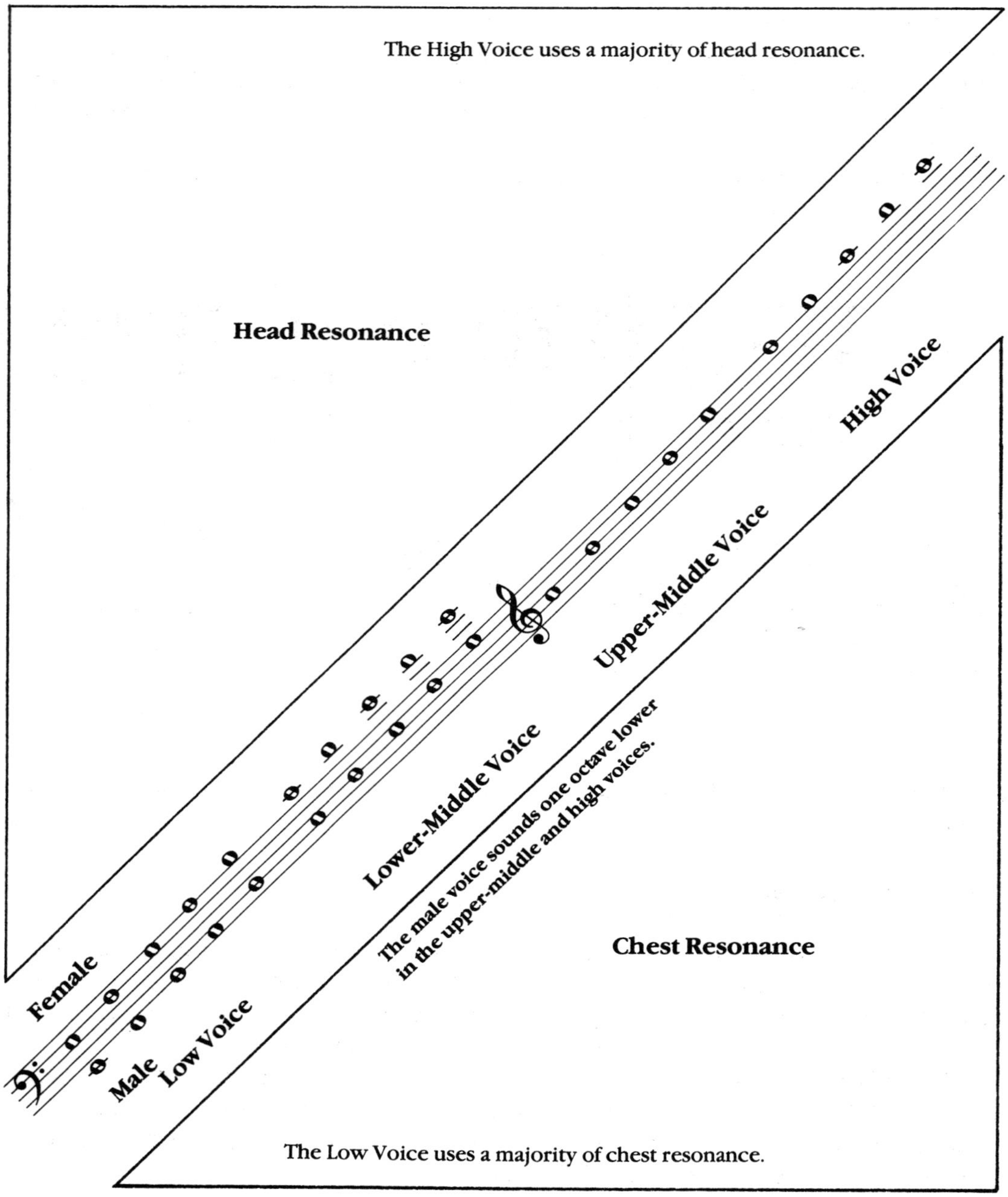

Basic Vowel Sounds

The next exercise is designed to help you produce your voice with consistency of quality throughout the range of a song. You will be using three vowels, "oh" (as in the word "owe"), "ah" (as in the word "art"), and "ee" (as in the word "eat").

Here is a diagram of how your lips should look when singing the basic vowel sounds. As you practice speaking these sounds, notice how your lips and jaw change position to produce each different vowel. As you will see, the quality and consistency of your singing voice depends on your ability to produce the basic vowel sounds correctly.

Basic Vowel Sounds

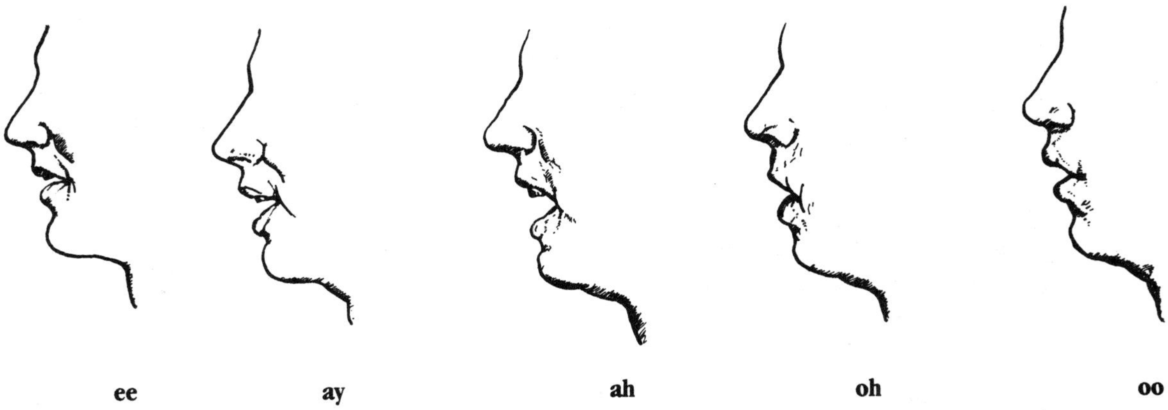

Begin by humming an "m" sound, as you did earlier. This time, follow the hum with a chanted "oh," "ah," and "ee," respectively.

Now try the vocal exercise. As you sing each vowel, enunciate clearly—just as if you were speaking very precisely.

Now try the same exercise, progressing up the *chromatic scale* by *half steps* through your range. The chromatic scale is always based on half steps (a half step is the distance from one note on the piano to the next note, whether black or white). Many of the exercises in this book are designed to be practiced in a chromatic sequence. Concentrate on keeping the quality of tone consistent as you sing each note. This will take some practice, so you should repeat this exercise several times. When singing vocal exercises, be sure your jaw is relaxed and your tongue is lying with the tip gently touching your lower teeth.

For additional practice, sing through "Here's That Rainy Day" on each of the three vowels, respectively. Listen to yourself and always aim to keep the quality of the tone consistent.

Intervals

When you sing through "Here's That Rainy Day" with the lyrics, you'll notice that some of the notes are more difficult to sing than others. An *interval* is the distance between two notes. Usually the most difficult notes to sing are in large intervals that progress up the scale by skips. This is because singing from low to high requires more *breath support* and more space inside your mouth than singing from high to low.

The following exercise will give you practice singing from high to low. When beginning with a high note, it is natural to create more space inside your mouth and to use more support. Before you begin, think the pitch, relax your jaw, and imagine that the tone begins across your head between your ears. The "k" sound will help you start the vowel on the pitch. Keep the tone as clear as possible.

The next exercise is based on measure 2 of the vocal line of "Here's That Rainy Day." This measure includes intervals that are difficult to sing. By learning this process, you can create similar exercises to help you with other songs that contain difficult notes or intervals. The intervals in "Here's That Rainy Day" are reversed in the first measure of this exercise to give you practice singing them from high to low. In the second measure, the intervals are as they appear in the song, from low to high.

Repeat this process for the difficult intervals in measure 6 of the song.

Now, sing the first two phrases of "Here's That Rainy Day" with the lyrics. You should find them much easier to sing than before. Remember to apply this practice technique to other songs.

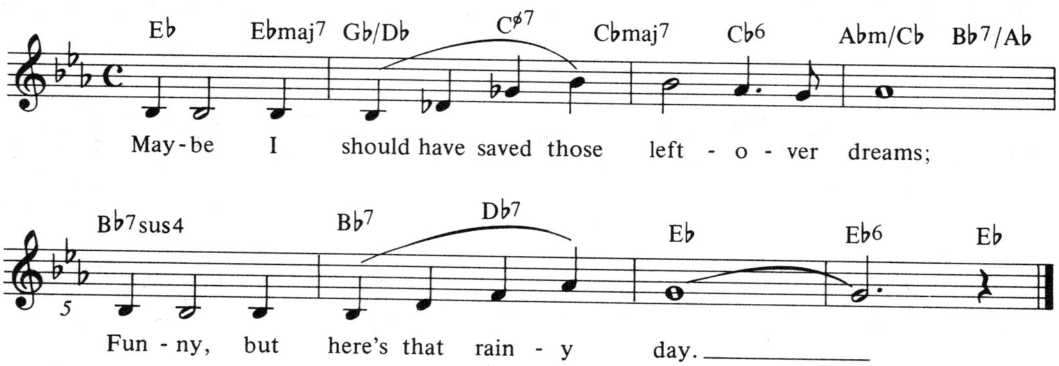

By now, you are familiar with "Here's That Rainy Day." You have practiced the quality of sound most often associated with popular singing styles—including pop, rock, rhythm and blues, and jazz. You have also learned how to produce this quality consistently in your middle voice.

Selecting Music

The next part of the vocal coaching session provides you with a practical method for selecting and approaching any new song. As you learn "Bye Bye Baby," you will also find out how to pinpoint difficult notes—and make them work to your best advantage. This section also covers some important rules of pronunciation that are essential to singers—and will teach you how to add vocal decorations to a song that can really bring out your personal performance style.

"Bye Bye Baby" was written for the Broadway musical *Gentlemen Prefer Blondes,* starring Carol Channing. Marilyn Monroe and Jane Russell starred in the film version and the musical later reopened on Broadway titled *Lorelei,* which again starred Carol Channing. Let's take a close look at the sheet music. The following information will help you select the songs you want to sing—and show you how to transpose a song into your key.

The *sheet music* of a popular song usually contains a vocal line and a simplified piano arrangement of the song. A *lead sheet* features the vocal line with the chord symbols only. (*Chord symbols* are a shorthand method for writing chords.) Many lead sheets also contain guitar fingering charts. Pianists and guitarists who are skilled in *improvisation* will create their own arrangement from the lead sheet as they go along. Improvisation is music which is created spontaneously—not written down. The lead sheet provides a musician with the song's basic melody and harmony, and the final arrangement is left to the discretion of the accompanying instrumentalist. Sheet music provides a piano arrangement which can be used by pianists who are not skilled in improvisation. It also usually contains the chord symbols—and often, also, the guitar fingering charts.

When songs are performed, the melody is seldom played in the accompaniment—although it is printed in the right hand of the piano part. The melody is included to make it easy to learn the song. It also allows the song to be played as an instrumental piece—that is, without a singer. The songs in this book contain complete piano arrangements, as well as chord symbols. If you are a guitar player or pianist, you can enjoy both playing and singing these songs—or you can work together with a friend who plays one of these instruments.

When you buy the sheet music of popular tunes, you will not get the arrangement you have heard on a recording. Recording artists have music arranged especially for them, and those arrangements are their personal property and seldom published. You may also find the sheet music is in a different key than the recording you have heard. The key chosen by the recording artist is that key which best suits his or her voice. The sheet music arrangement is usually in a key that is easy to play and can be sung by most people. The term *key* refers to the *key signature,* which is the sharps or flats located at the beginning of the song. As a singer, you are concerned with the range of notes required by a given song. If the high notes are too high, the key must be lowered. If the low notes are too low, the key must be raised. If the song is both too high and too low, you would be advised to select another song with less range.

Transposing

When you sing through a song, you can decide if the song is too low or too high for you and then *transpose* it, if necessary. Transposing means to change the key of a song. If you are singing with a pianist who is a jazz or pop musician, he or she should be able to read chord symbols. This means that you will only have to change the chord symbols on the lead sheet in order to enable your accompanist to play the song in a new key.

In this example from "Bye Bye Baby," the chord symbols have been moved up one whole-step—from the key of B♭ to the key of C.

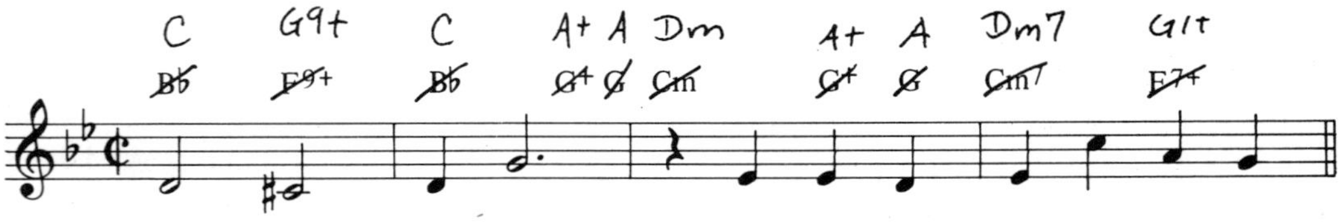

If your accompanist is not familiar with reading chord symbols, you will have to have someone write out the song in your key. This version of the song should contain both the vocal line and the accompaniment, as shown in the following example. All notes in this example have been moved up two whole-steps to the key of D. With some practice, you can transpose and recopy songs yourself.

Key of B♭

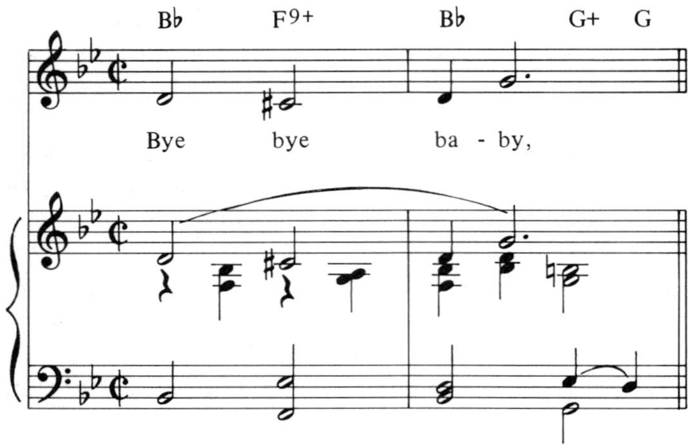

Key of D

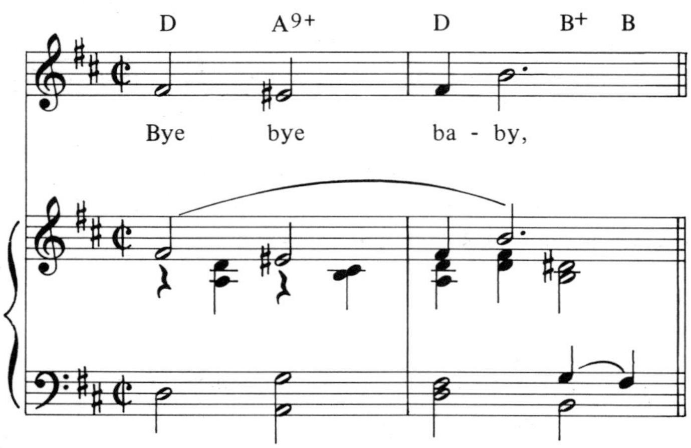

Pronunciation

Let's take a look at some words that are often mispronounced by singers. Turn to the section "Song Arrangements" and sing through "Bye Bye Baby" until you are familiar with it. After singing the song, take a look at the words "that you" and "won't you" in measures 9 and 10 of the vocal line.

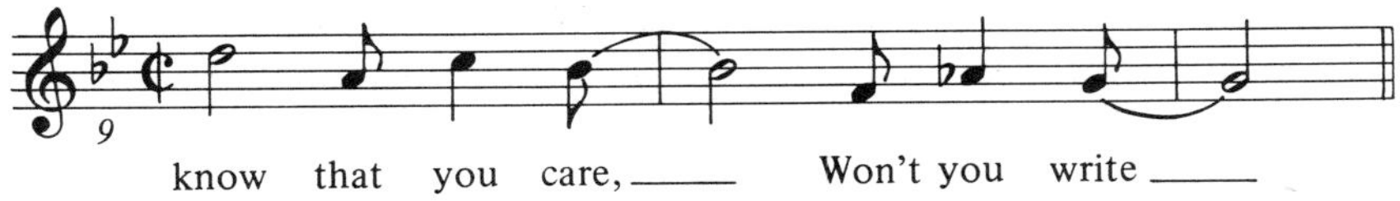

Singers commonly sing "tha-chew" for "that you" and "won-chew" for "won't you." The most common error made by Americans when singing consonants is to neglect final consonants, especially if they are explosives, like the letter "t." (See the section "Consonants" for a complete explanation of difficult consonant combinations.)

Practice speaking the words in measures 9 and 10, being careful to pronounce "that" and "won't" with the final "t."

One other pronunciation problem found in this song is caused when a consonant follows the vowel "i." This occurs in the common contractions "I'll" and "I'm." The contraction "I'll" can be found in measures 17 and 28 of the first verse and in measures 14, 17, 24, and 28 of the second verse. "I'm" can be found in measures 13 and 20 of the second verse. "I'll" and "I'm" are often mispronounced "all" and "ahm," respectively. When you speak the letter "i," you say "eye." When the "ll" or "m" is added, you should say "eye-ll" or "eye-m."

Practice these measures by pronouncing the words correctly out loud. For a further discussion of vowel sounds, refer to the section "Vowels."

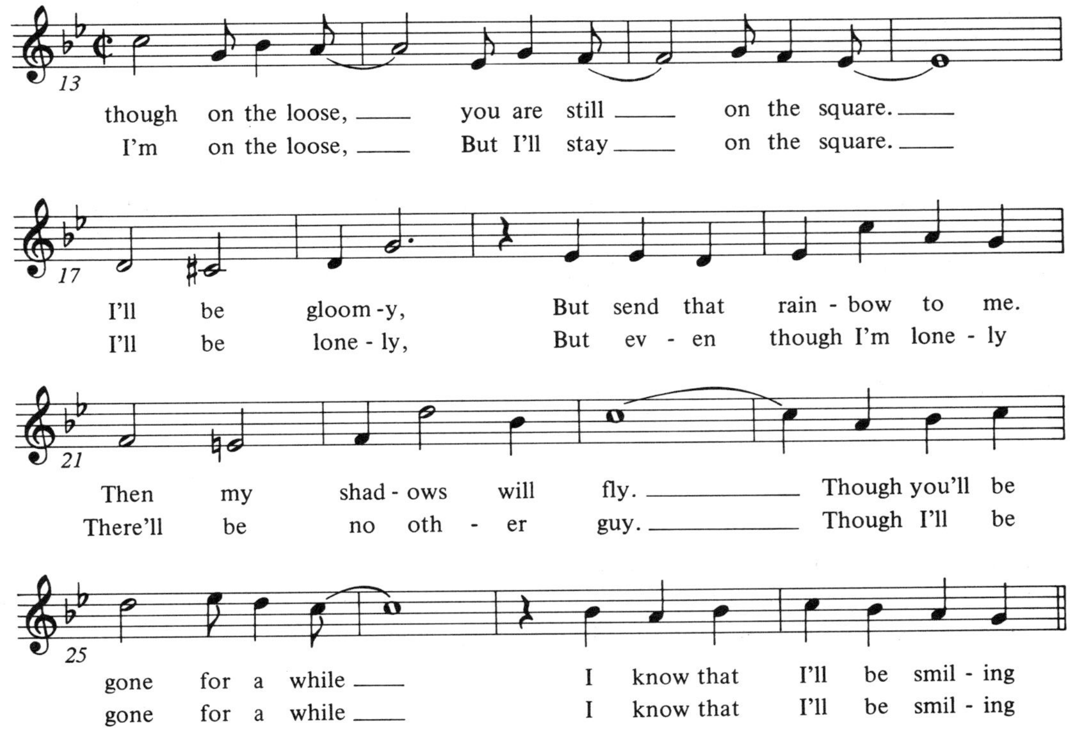

Embellishments

In the performance of popular music, most vocal artists add *embellishments* to songs. Embellishments are notes added to a melody. These are often written by song arrangers, but are sometimes added by the singers themselves.

Because jazz is an improvisational art form, jazz singers frequently add embellishments as they go along. Pop singers look for songs that are versatile and can be molded to their own personality or singing style. Some melodies can be improved with embellishment—and these often become popular hits.

As a singer, you must avoid creating your own arrangement before you are thoroughly familiar with the composer's melody and harmony. Think of improvisation as a chef considers creating masterpieces in food. If you are thoroughly familiar with the basic ingredients, then your addition of spices, herbs, or other ingredients will enhance a recipe. If you are not sure of the basic ingredients, you will not be able to create an appetizing dish.

In "Here's That Rainy Day," you practiced singing intervals (or skips). In "Bye Bye Baby," there are some intervals that are larger than those found in "Here's That Rainy Day." These intervals are found in measures 2, 4, 6, 12, 18, 20, and 22. You can tackle large intervals by focusing attention on the beginning consonant of the word that occurs on the high note of the interval. A singer must be certain to put that consonant on the pitch. Slurring, scooping, and sliding are usually the result of failure to do this.

Sometimes scoops and slides are intentionally added by a singer as embellishments to a song melody. Look at the first syllable of the word "baby" in measure 2. At this point in the song, a slide could be added to give the song a sultry quality.

In measure 4, the words "you're my" could be sung in a similar way. To capitalize on the natural scoop, you could add a *grace note* on the word "my." This grace note should be sung as quickly as possible. First practice singing the "m" right on the pitch. Then try it with a grace-note scoop.

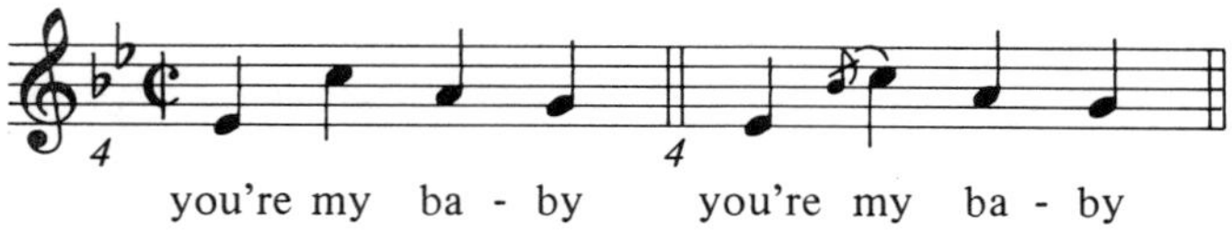

In measure 6, the words "give you" lend themselves to a sultry slur. This is because the word "you" is pronounced "ee-oo." You can read more about this in the section "Double Vowel Sounds." (If you wish to avoid this natural slur, you must put the "ee" sound on the pitch.)

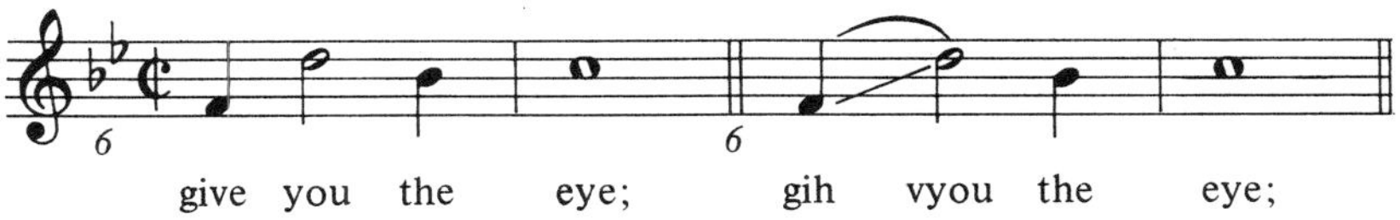

In measure 12, you can create a slide by connecting the words "declare" and "that."

When you sing the word "gloomy" in measure 18, you can slide up on the "oo" sound and put the "m" on the top note. (If you wish to avoid this slide, be careful that the "oo" occurs on the low note only.)

In measure 20, you can create a jazzy effect by humming up on the "n" sound in the word "rainbow."

In measure 22, the first syllable of the word "shadows" could be slurred upward. (It is fairly easy to put the "d" on the top note if you wish to avoid this slide.)

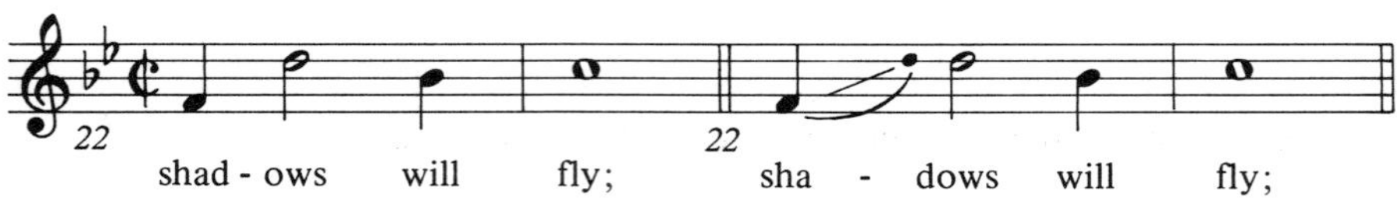

Each of these examples illustrates how you can embellish large intervals when singing a song. Remember, if you purposely plan the slide or slur for effect, that is fine. It is when the slides are sung by accident that they usually sound like mistakes.

Sing through "Bye Bye Baby" several times. As you do this, practice singing the large intervals with the embellishments you have learned, as well as without them. This particular song offers the singer considerable creative stylistic leeway. As you work on any new song, find an interpretation that fits your personality and go with it.

Using Consonants

Articulation is the action of the speech organs in the formation of consonants and vowels which make up individual syllables and words. The singer who pronounces consonants clearly is seldom misunderstood. That's why it pays to devote regular practice time to this important aspect of articulation.

The consonants that are produced in the front of the mouth are the easiest consonants to sing, especially at a rapid speed. Here is an exercise containing some of them. Practice it by firmly articulating the consonants as you sing the notes.

Here is another consonant exercise. This one alternates consonants produced in the front of the mouth with those produced in the back.

♩ = 132
poh kah boh gah
foh scha voh djah
simile

Now turn to the section "Song Arrangements" and sing through "Personality," paying special attention to clear articulation. This rhythm song was sung by Johnny Mercer, Bing Crosby, and Pearl Bailey, among others. Remember that singing requires much more exaggerated articulation than speaking. As a singer, you must be understood by a large audience. Whether you have a microphone or not, clarity of articulation is very important. If the audience does not understand the lyrics, you have not communicated with them. Always remember—a song is not a song without lyrics.

Using a Microphone

Popular singing is almost always performed with a microphone. The microphone only amplifies sound. It will not improve or clarify your voice. Your articulation has to be just as precise as if you were singing without the microphone. Louis Armstrong, Carol Channing, and Eartha Kitt are three exceptional performers who have unusual vocal qualities—and who understand how to communicate lyrics to an audience. Consider listening to recordings by these artists.

Comic Delivery

In every singing style, communication with the audience is more important than anything else. Communication invokes understanding—and this process relies on the singer's articulation of consonants. Your ability to communicate is particularly important when singing a comic song like "Personality."

Sing through "Personality" again. This time, make an effort to tell the story of the lyric as though you are making it up as you go along. The first verse is written for a male singer and the second verse is written for a female singer. You may enjoy performing this song as a duet with a friend of the opposite sex.

This kind of rhythm song owes its heritage to the comic operas of Gilbert and Sullivan. If you are interested in musical theater, you will enjoy singing their songs as well as other rhythm songs—especially if you like to captivate an audience with comedy.

Phrasing and Dynamics

No discussion of songs would be complete without mentioning phrasing, dynamics, and form. A *phrase* is a musical or lyrical group of notes or words that create a satisfying feeling. Several phrases are needed to create a feeling of completeness in a song. In a well-written song, each *musical phrase* is designed to fit exactly with each *lyrical phrase.*

In "Here's That Rainy Day," the musical and lyrical phrases are the same and pose no problem for the singer. As you sing each phrase of the song, your voice will naturally get louder (*crescendo*) and then softer (*diminuendo*). The different levels of volume in a song are known as its *dynamics.* Although some singers may choose a different *interpretation* (or approach to the song)—the phrasing and dynamics marked in this lead sheet of "Here's That Rainy Day" are the natural choice. Note that the curved lines (also called *phrase marks*) outline the first two phrases of the song. Crescendo signs ($<$) and diminuendo signs ($>$) show where your voice should get louder and softer, respectively.

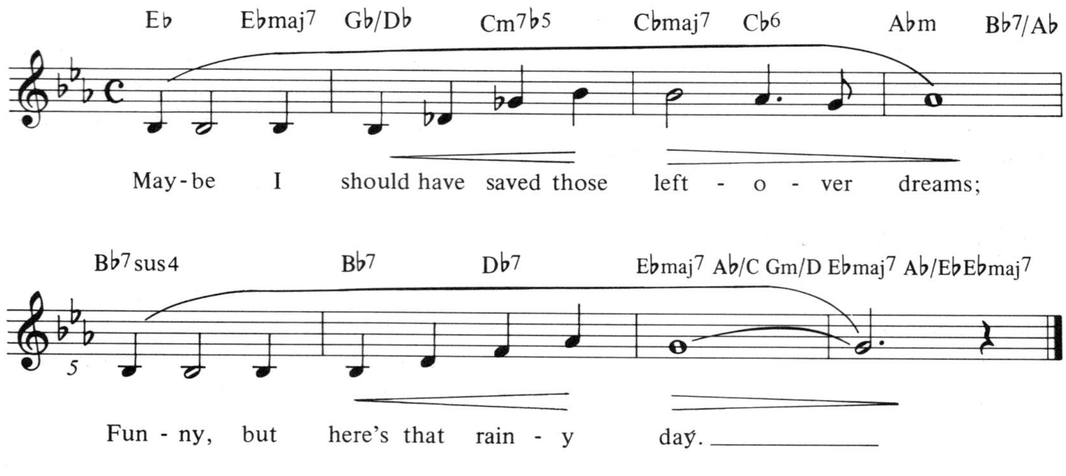

In "Bye Bye Baby," an extended lyrical phrase occurs in measures 8 through 16. However, the musical phrase changes in measure 12 between the words "declare" and "that."

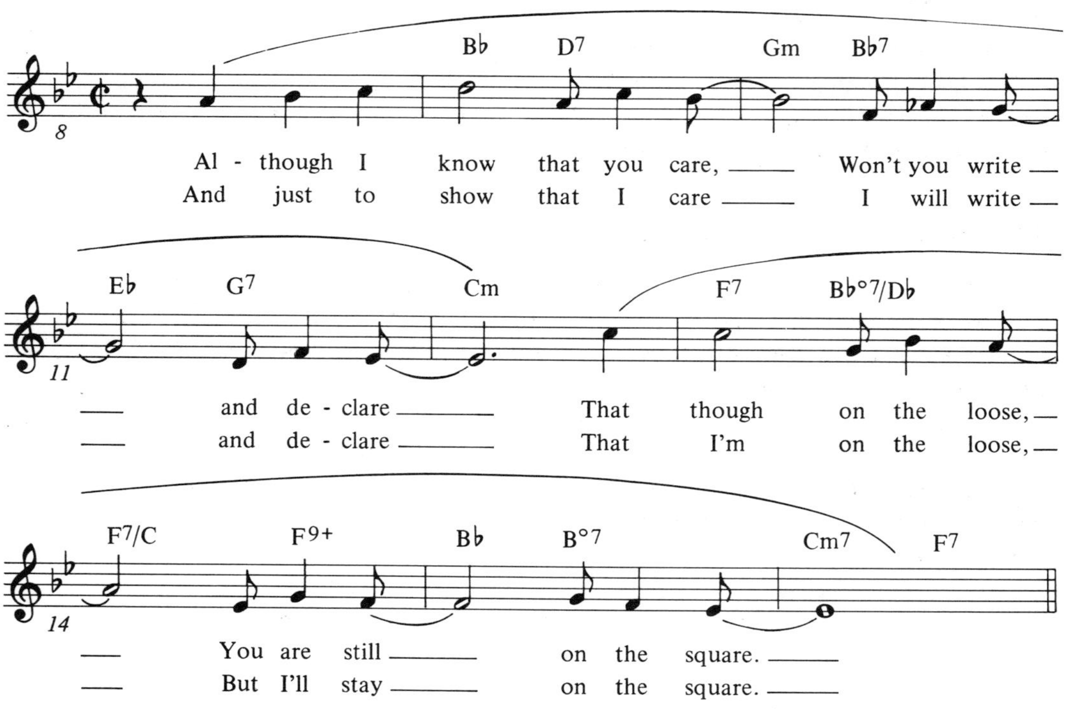

Song Form

Taken together, the phrases of a song outline its form. The traditional *song form* calls for thirty-two bars (or *measures*), arranged in four eight-bar sections. Once you are able to recognize the form of a song you will also be aware of its patterns of repetition. Each different musical section is assigned a letter name—*A, B, C,* and so on. Similar musical sections are assigned the same name. This system provides a convenient shorthand for notating the form of a song. For example, "Personality" is in AABA form, while "Here's That Rainy Day" is in ABAC form. Thousands of other songs are based on these standard patterns.

Each section of a song contains one or more phrases. Although the standard section contains eight bars, this number may vary. Individual sections are sometimes called *eight,* because they often consist of eight bars. Thus, the first and second eight in AABA song form are A sections, the third eight is the B section, and the fourth eight is an A section. In AABA song form, the B section is also called the *bridge* (or *release*). However, in ABAB song form, there is no bridge. The third section is simply referred to as the third eight.

Many songs and song arrangements feature variations on standard forms. Although "Here's That Rainy Day" is in ABAC form, the arrangement in this book also features a two-bar extended instrumental ending. Some songs use more unusual song forms. "Bye Bye Baby" is in ABAC form with an eight-bar extended vocal ending. "Personality" follows the typical AABA form with standard eight-bar phrases.

Country, Folk, and Blues

Many singers wish to develop their ability to sing different vocal styles. The next sections will provide you with background about the most popular of today's singing styles—and some important tips about how to make them work for you.

Country, folk, and blues songs often rely on the personal tone of the singer for their emotional impact. These songs feature lyrics that tell a specific story, from a personal perspective. When singing these styles, your vocal tone should be friendly and appealing, with appropriate colloquial pronunciation. Nasal consonants are usually nasalized to produce the soft "twang" associated with country, folk, and blues music. The accompaniment in these styles is usually fairly sparse—and, for this reason, the vocalist does not need to produce a high level of volume. The best way to learn the nuances of country singing is to listen to some great country singers, such as Merle Haggard and Dolly Parton. For those singers who wish to learn more about the blues, listen to classic greats like Bessie Smith and B. B. King. If you are interested in folk music, listen to recordings by Simon & Garfunkel, Judy Collins, or Don McLean. If you are a country or folk singer, you will enjoy singing the Simon & Garfunkel hit, "Scarborough Fair." Turn to the piano/vocal arrangement of this song in the "Song Arrangements" section at the end of your book and sing through this popular ballad.

Rock

Rock music relies on drama to put across its message. This drama has been expressed in every theatrical form imaginable: sets, costumes, makeup, lighting, sound, movement, and music. Many rock singers both play the guitar and sing. Rock music has explored and developed the extremes of the human voice.

Falsetto

Falsetto is a legitimate vocal sound in rock music—and is used extensively by male rock stars. The term falsetto refers to the high range which occurs above the normal range of the male voice. If you are a male vocalist, when singing up the scale, you will move from a note that matches the rest of your voice to several notes that sound light and perhaps breathy. Above this range, your voice becomes clear again and will sound like the voice of a soprano. With practice, the breathy notes can be made clear. When this range is developed, it is sometimes called *reinforced falsetto.* This scale shows approximately where the falsetto notes lie. Some of the notes marked "Reinforced Falsetto" may be sung either in falsetto or regular voice.

Written Notes

Actual Notes Sung

You can see that the male voice sounds an *octave* (or eight notes) lower than written. You probably already know that, while song melodies are written in the *treble clef* (𝄞), the male singer should sing them an octave lower. The ability to sing falsetto varies from person to person. However, like all parts of the voice, the falsetto range can be developed with study and practice.

The arrangement of "There Are Such Things" in the section "Song Arrangements" is provided as a study in falsetto for male singers. Although female singers may wish to add this great song to their repertoire, the instructions that accompany this tune will not be applicable. However, the next section is devoted to belting—and should be quite helpful.

Male singers use falsetto to create a special effect at selected points in a song. Turn to the arrangement of "There Are Such Things" and take a look at the points in the song where reinforced falsetto and high falsetto are indicated. As you sing through the song, try to change smoothly from your normal range to falsetto range. Your ability to do this will improve each time you practice "There Are Such Things." Here is an exercise that will help you develop your falsetto range.

Falsetto (like a sigh)

Experiment with falsetto range as you sing other songs. Add falsetto where it seems appropriate and try to make changes in range sound natural and smooth.

Broadway

Broadway music includes all styles of singing. The musicals by Rodgers and Hammerstein, such as *The Sound of Music* and *Carousel,* require primarily legitimate vocal quality. Many more recent musicals, such as *Little Shop of Horrors* and *Cats* are written in pop style. *Dream Girls* features Motown-style music, while *Hair* and *Jesus Christ Superstar* are considered rock musicals.

"Diamonds Are a Girl's Best Friend" is a very showy number that has been recorded by many talented stars—including Eartha Kitt, Pearl Bailey, Ethel Merman, and Emmylou Harris. This song provides an excellent study for female singers who wish to master the art of belting.

Belting

Belting is an important technique used in Broadway musicals, particularly for female singers. In simple terms, *belting* is supported and controlled yelling. When belting, a very powerful stream of air is directed at the vocal cords. Dancers are often good belters because they have strong abdominal muscles.

Proper belting is not harmful to your voice. However, if your voice becomes tired when belting, you should stop immediately. Unlike the larger muscles of the body, the vocal cords are sensitive. In other words, the expression "no pain, no gain" does not apply to the human voice. Before beginning to belt, be sure your voice is warmed up (as you did before singing "Here's That Rainy Day").

Successful belting is largely dependent on your ability to support your breath. Here's an exercise you can practice to feel the deep support needed in belting. Imagine that you are frightened and calling for help. The nearest person is a block away and you must make him hear you. Take a breath deep enough that you can yell "Hey!" and be heard a block away. Now, shout a long "Ha-a-a-a-y."

The Diaphragm

Let's examine the breathing process that takes place when you do this exercise. The *diaphragm* is a muscular plate that separates the chest cavity from the abdominal cavity. If you are fully supporting your voice, you will feel your diaphragm lower when you take a breath, as shown in the diagram.

Front View of Lungs With Diaphragm

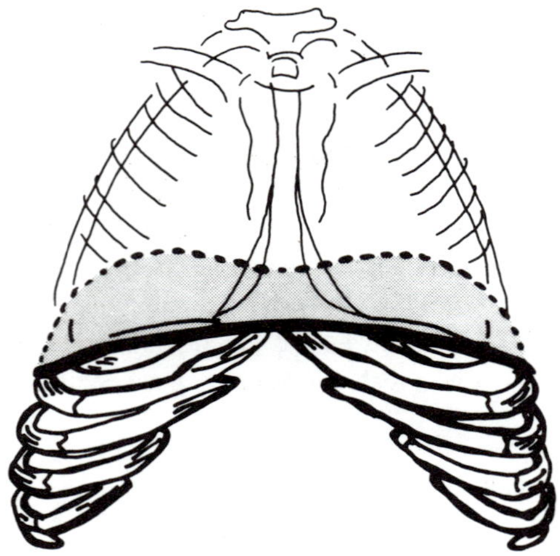

--- = diaphragm when lower lungs are not filled with air

— = diaphragm when lower lungs are filled with air

As you take in breath, you should also feel your rib cage and abdomen expand, as shown in this diagram.

Side View of Body

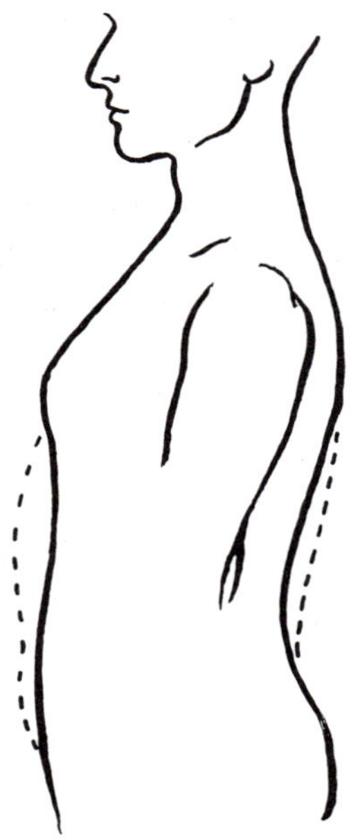

The dotted lines show the expansion of the rib cage when the lower lungs are filled with air.

When you shout "Hay," it should sound as though you are holding a long note. You should not feel the sound in your throat. Once you can accomplish this, you will be able to belt.

The exercise and song that follow are arranged to provide the female singer with practice in belting. Male belting is a legitimate vocal style, produced similarly to female belting. For the female singer, belting is a common requirement of rock, pop, and Broadway music. At this point, male singers may wish to turn back to "There Are Such Things," for additional practice singing falsetto. The female singer should practice the following belting exercise—and then practice belting "Diamonds Are a Girl's Best Friend."

Female singers should now turn to the section "Song Arrangements," and learn the lyrics and melody of "Diamonds Are a Girl's Best Friend." The vocal line of this arrangement lies in a comfortable low belting range. It may seem somewhat low to you at first—but, for practice purposes, it is best not to belt too high. When you are familiar with this number, practice belting through the entire song. Once you know it fairly well, you can enjoy performing it for your friends. If you learn to sing this song with meaning and confidence, you'll find it makes a great audition piece, too.

During this vocal coaching session, you have learned some important vocal techniques and musical terms. You can apply your knowledge of lyrics, pitch, and song form to any new song you wish to sing—and experiment with different vocal techniques along the way as you discover your own personal singing style. You are now ready to move on to a step-by-step voice lesson. Enjoy your new skills, and remember, "perfect practice makes perfect."

Daily Vocal Warmup

Here's a series of vocal exercises designed to build up important parts of your voice. If you practice this daily vocal warmup once every day, you will soon notice that your voice is able to respond easily and clearly. You will also find that you can sing for a longer period of time without tiring.

Since the vocal cords are muscles, they should be exercised—and warmup will prepare you for long periods of vocal exertion. Rock singers, in particular, need to warm up to avoid injury to their voices. After hard singing, it is also valuable to warm down with this series of exercises. This will allow your vocal cords to return to normal gradually and easily. Dancers have found a good warmdown valuable after a concert or strenuous class. Because the vocal muscles are more delicate than other muscles in the body, singers require warmups and warmdowns even more than dancers and athletes.

Vocal Warmup

kah
koh
kee
simile
ee ee ee ee ee
oh oh oh oh oh
ah ah ah ah ah
simile

yah yah yah yah yah yah yah
simile
lah lah lah lah lah lah lah lah lah lah lah lah lah
lay lay lay lay lay lay lay lay lay lay lay lay lay
loh loh loh loh loh loh loh loh loh loh loh loh loh
simile

Voice Lesson

The study of voice can be a thrilling experience, or an exercise in frustration. Your understanding and approach may determine which experience you will have. Everyone who sings has a different background and a different vocal instrument. Today, almost any person with vocal talent can be successful—provided he or she has a good ear and is a consummate performer. The ability to please and entertain an audience is true communication. However, your vocal technique must be good enough to express your meaning clearly and attractively in word and music.

For the singer, practicing the basics of singing is comparable to the dancer working at the bar. The dancer trains in basic positions to assure that the muscles are properly exercised and that the body is in perfect alignment. This training is valuable to all dancers—not just ballet dancers. In the same way, practicing the basics of singing is valuable to all vocalists—no matter what style of singing they prefer. In fact, learning the basics of singing and correct practice will help your voice more than you can imagine.

Some students are turned off to studying voice because they feel they are not learning what they want to learn. Now that you've had the chance to perform some songs in a vocal coaching session, you will benefit from learning some more of the basics in the voice lesson. The exercises in this lesson will provide you with valuable practice material for future vocal study. Repeat these exercises regularly, as you continue to add new songs to your repertoire.

The singing of exercises is also called *vocalizing.* A good voice lesson includes exercises and songs. In years past, some teachers only allowed their students to sing exercises for several years until they felt they were ready to sing songs. This approach requires consistent study for a number of years—and only works for the most determined and trusting students. Needless to say, this method has nearly disappeared.

Today's philosophy is much more immediate—and has almost neglected vocal study altogether. The rock culture has expanded the vocalist's performance to include light shows, special effects, movement, and electronic sounds. In rock videos, the senses are further tantalized with art, camera work, and dance. These effects have all become equally as important as the quality of the human voice. Nevertheless, learning to sing correctly will help you become stronger and gain facility in singing any style. It will also help you protect your voice from abuse.

The Head Voice

When you studied pop placement in the first part of this book, you learned to focus vocal tones in the front of your mouth. Now, as you expand your range, you will learn to keep the high tones in the back of your mouth and bring your head voice into the middle register. This means that your voice will sound lighter as you come down the scale. Try to accomplish this each time you practice this exercise. When you begin to feel the difference in the two ways of focusing the tone, you can practice both styles.

When you focus vocal tone in the back of the mouth, you are using your head voice. This technique is based on a singing style developed during the Renaissance in Italy called *bel canto* (which, in Italian, means "beautiful singing"). Popular singers of the thirties and forties used this style because they were classically trained. However, today's pop singers use the placement you learned when you worked on "Here's That Rainy Day" in the vocal coaching session. It is important to understand the difference between these two different vocal techniques. If you listen to recordings by the Andrews Sisters, you will hear legitimate tone quality. Compare this with the pop placement used by the Supremes and you will immediately hear the difference between the two styles of vocal production.

You are already familiar with vowels and consonants. Speaking and rapid singing capitalize on consonant sounds, while slow and sustained singing relies on vowels. The English language has several pronunciations for each vowel. In classical singing, vowels are based on those of the Italian language, which offers one basic pronunciation for each vowel.

Let's begin to develop your head voice by focusing on three important vowel sounds—"ah," "oh," and "ee"—which are produced using *head resonance* (also called *head voice*). First, pronounce "ah," "oh," and "ee." Articulate these vowels in your *larynx* (or *voice box*). The sounds should be clear and resonant.

In the following exercise, the consonant "k" has been added before each of these vowels. This consonant is produced between the back of the tongue and the roof of the mouth. This exercise is similar to one that you worked on in the vocal coaching session to practice singing from high to low. Here, the exercise will help you articulate the vowel on the high note and assist you in lifting the roof of your mouth (or *palate*) to the optimum position. The technical term for this movement is *raising the palate*. You should feel as though you are about to sneeze when you lift your palate in this way. This lift also helps create the space needed inside your mouth to produce the high note at the beginning of each measure. When you breathe, before and during this exercise, try to raise your palate so that the air feels cool on the roof of your mouth.

As you continue to practice this exercise, try to sing the top note as clearly as possible. If you must sing it falsetto, this is okay for now. It is important to get used to raising the palate and to become familiar with the shape of your mouth as you sing each vowel. Make the vowels sound as pure as possible. Once you have mastered this, try this variation. Practice it first with the "k" sounds, as written. Then try the exercise without the "k" sounds.

Try this exercise once again—this time, as you come down the scale, imagine you are going down in an elevator. Try to produce the bottom notes in the same way as the top notes.

Regular practice of the previous exercise will help you develop strength in the low part of your head voice. If you progress too low, you will automatically shift into your chest voice. Practice the exercise, moving lower until you feel the change in quality. (Singers with high voices will usually experience more quality change than those with low voices.)

Posture

If you were slumping or sitting back when you tried these exercises, you undoubtedly discovered that you need to either sit upright or stand in order to sing them with ease. This is because the high notes need added breath support—which is only possible in these upright body positions. Most students stand during voice lessons. You'll find that standing allows your body to assume the most perfect position for breathing while singing.

To assume a good standing posture, try this exercise. Stretch toward the ceiling with your arms above your head, with your hands interlocked and palms facing upward. Now, keeping your body tall, relax your arms at your sides. The stretch should have tightened your abdominal muscles. Relax your shoulders, but don't let them droop. Tighten your buttocks. If your shoulders feel tense, move them up and back, and then let them rest in place. Your feet should be firmly planted on the ground with your toes turned outward slightly. If you are standing correctly, you should be able to lift your toes up and down without throwing yourself off balance. Your chin should be parallel to the floor and your neck should be lengthened in back.

Holding good posture feels very awkward when you have held your body out of alignment for years. Once you have learned good posture, you will gradually discover how much better you feel and how much better you can sing.

Check your posture when you are walking down the street. Look at your hands. If your thumbs are facing forward, your shoulders are in alignment. If your thumbs are facing your body, your shoulders are drooping. Just roll your shoulders back and feel the difference. The proper alignment of your body frees all of its parts to function without tension. The less tension you have, the freer your voice will be.

Assume a good standing posture and try this exercise. You may find your volume has increased considerably.

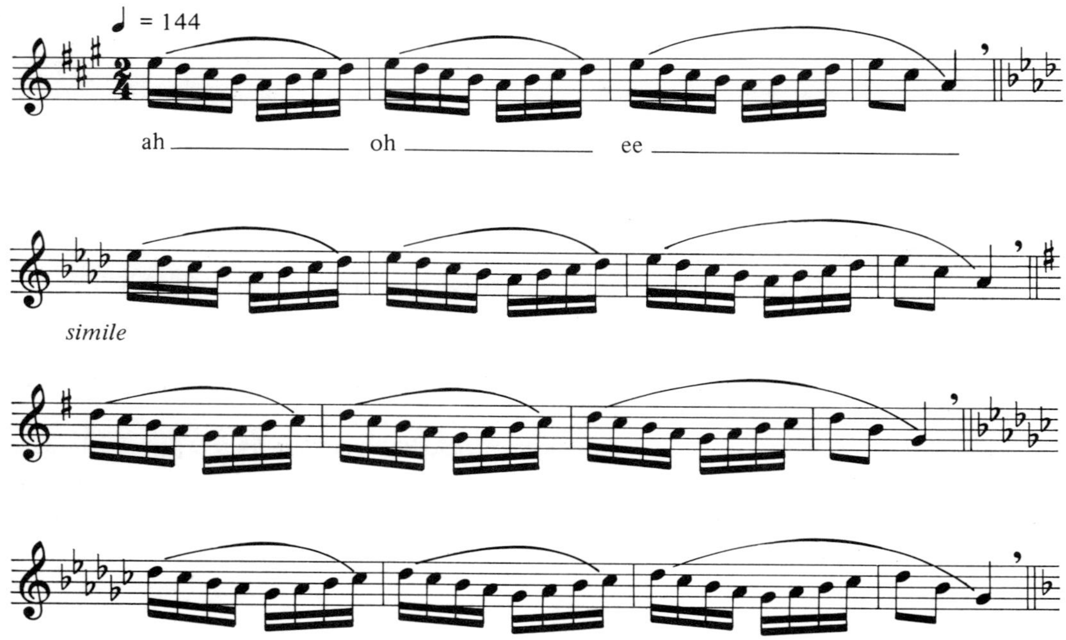

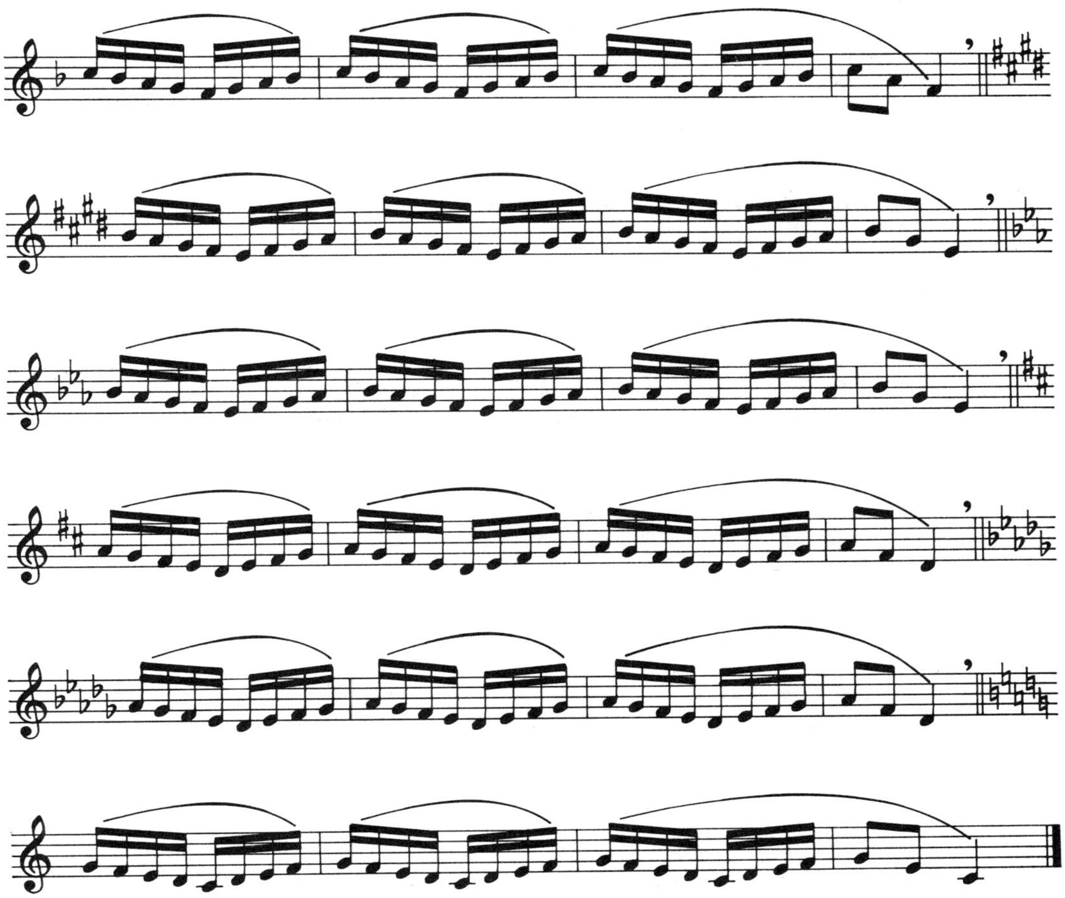

Staccato

One of the most valuable vocal techniques to practice is *staccato.* Staccato notes are marked with a dot above or below the notehead. Each staccato note should be short and light when sung. Practicing staccato technique will help you develop good breath support. Your ability to sing staccato is also a good gauge of the health of your voice. If your voice is tired, if you have a cold, or if you have misused your voice, you may not be able to sing staccato notes. If this is the case, it is advisable to rest your voice for a few days. If the problem persists, see a throat doctor.

As you sing this simple staccato exercise, make the notes as short and light as possible. You will feel your diaphragm pulse with each note. Notice the first vowel sound of the exercise is "ee." The "ee" sound makes it easy to sing a staccato on a low note. (For most people, this is a difficult vowel to sustain on a high note.)

♩ = 160
ee ee ee ee oh oh oh oh ah ah ah ah ah
simile

Legato

Unlike the short, light staccato notes, *legato* notes are connected and smooth—and should be held for their full note value. A good and balanced vocal warmup should include alternating staccato and legato exercises. These two techniques require the use of different sets of muscles. As you sing this exercise, be sure to differentiate between staccato and legato notes, as marked.

The Throat and Jaw

You already know the importance of the raised palate (sometimes called the "inner smile"). You have probably noticed that, when you raise the palate, you stretch the back of your throat. In order to sing powerful high notes, you need a very flexible throat and jaw. The next exercise is also a throat stretcher. As you practice this exercise, imagine you are chewing caramels with your back teeth and move your jaw as much as possible. It looks ridiculous, but this is a valuable exercise that combines use of mouth space with good breath support.

As you continue to practice this exercise, you may notice that the higher notes will begin to take on the deep quality of the low notes. This addition of chest resonance to the head voice is the basis of operatic vocal production.

Articulation

As you know, the best way to involve an audience in your performance is to articulate the lyrics of a song clearly. In your vocal coaching session, you learned the importance of consonants to good articulation—and how consonants help set vowels into motion. The next exercise combines vowels and consonants and requires good breath support. Be sure to articulate each sound clearly.

So far, you have learned to sing downward scales in your head voice. You have practiced staccato and legato technique and learned exercises to help you stretch your throat and jaw.

The Tongue

The tongue is another important part of your vocal mechanism. This next exercise will help make your tongue more flexible. Sing the exercise slowly and carefully at first. Each time you repeat this exercise, sing it at a faster *tempo* (or speed). Your final goal should be to sing the exercise as quickly as possible. (For additional practice, try the exercise on "lay" and "loh.")

As you know, slow singing is sustained on vowel sounds. In this lesson, you have focused on four vowel sounds, "ah," "ay," "ee," and "oh." These four vowel sounds are the most commonly used vowels for vocalization. However, to develop the full potential of your voice, you need to practice all the vowels. Read the section "Vowels" for a detailed discussion of each of these.

The next exercise includes nine different vowel sounds. As you sing this exercise, remember to use good breath support. You will notice that, as you sing higher, you need more breath.

ah ee oo ih
oh ay aw eh uh
ah ah ee oo
ih oh ay aw eh
uh ah ah ee
oo ih oh ay aw
eh uh ah ah
ee oo ih oh ay
aw eh uh ah

To perfect this exercise, articulate each vowel sound clearly and be sure the tone quality is consistent through the entire range of your voice. When you can sing the sequence three times on one breath without stopping, you will have mastered *breath control,* which is the ability to conserve breath over long passages of music.

As you come across problems in songs, learn to create your own exercises to solve them. The exercises you create will differ from the exercises you have learned in this lesson—because they will incorporate parts of a song melody rather than general patterns and scales. You'll find that your voice will welcome the difficult passages in songs once you have isolated and practiced them in useful exercises.

Singing, when done well, is a very satisfying experience. It produces a natural high which is created by the breath as it oxygenates the blood, improves the circulation, strengthens health, and gives one an overall feeling of elation.

You now have a working knowledge of vocal technique. When you combine good vocal technique, an understanding of musical styles, and performance ability, your charismatic personality will make you welcome in the hearts of audiences everywhere.

Technical Guidelines for Singers

The section that follows provides a detailed explanation of consonants, vowels, and breathing. You have already learned something about these important aspects of singing. Now, you will have the opportunity to learn them in greater detail. This section will also be a valuable reference as you learn new songs and continue your study of voice.

Consonants

Consonants can be mysterious creatures to singers because there are so many of them—and because they may be combined with vowels in so many different ways. Confusion regarding consonants can result in singing that is either difficult to understand or that sounds affected. Neither effect is desirable.

Consonants are logically grouped according to the way in which they're formed by the teeth, lips, and tongue. This section will present the consonants and consonant sounds in the order of their importance to the singer—that is, in terms of the relative difficulty of their pronunciation.

Nasal Consonants

The consonants that are most troublesome are those on which sound can be sustained—*l, m, n,* and *r.* These are called *nasal consonants,* because they are produced with pure nasal resonance. Nasal consonants can create problems relating to the production of the vowel that follows them.

In the song "No Other Love" from *Me and Juliet* by Rodgers and Hammerstein, there are many examples of these sustained consonants.

No other love have I	(no, love)
Only my love for you	(only, my, love, for)
Only the dream we knew	(only, dream, knew)

These three lines feature all the nasal consonants—*l, m, n,* and *r.* These are also called *hummed consonants,* because they are produced with a hummed nasal resonance. You can prove this by holding your nose and trying to sustain any one of these consonants. When the nasal cavities are closed off in this way, you will not be able to articulate these hummed consonant sounds.

When a nasal consonant is followed by a vowel, the singer must avoid the tendency to sing the vowel with too much nasal resonance. In the excerpt from "No Other Love," the words "no," "love," "my," and "only" are subject to this problem. To sing these words correctly, you must be sure to sing a pure vowel sound after each nasal consonant.

Vowel Consonants

In "No Other Love," there are two other consonants on which sound can be sustained—"y" and "w." These consonants are sometimes called *vowel consonants* because, although they may serve as consonants, they are produced by singing vowel sounds. The letter "y" is pronounced as the vowel sound "ee." So, for example, the word "you" is actually pronounced "ee-oo."

The vowel consonant "w" is produced with the vowel sound "oo." So the word "we" is pronounced with two vowel sounds, "oo-ee." (The section "Double Vowel Sounds" provides a further explanation of how these vowel consonants are sung.)

The consonants "d" and "t" must be articulated with care when followed by the vowel consonant "y." Consider the word "you" as used in "If I Loved You" from *Carousel* by Rodgers and Hammerstein. When singing "loved you," singers sometimes blend the two distinct sounds "d" and "y" into a single "j" sound (they mistakenly sing "love-joo" instead of "loved ee-oo"). A similar problem occurs when the consonant "t" is followed by the vowel consonant "y." Avoid the mistake of blending these two distinct sounds into a "ch" sound. For example, consider the words "that you" and "won't you" in "Bye, Bye Baby."

> Although I know that you care
> Won't you write and declare

Singers should avoid blending "t" and "y" into a "ch" sound, as shown.

> Although I know tha-chew care
> Won-chew write and declare

As an exercise, look through any song you wish to sing and identify all of the nasal and vowel consonants: *l, m, n, r, w,* and *y.* Make a note of their placement in the vocal line—and determine which vowel sounds they precede. When you sing the song, remember to use pure vowel sounds after nasal consonants and avoid blending consonants together.

If you ever have difficulty singing a particular word in a song, make up a vocal exercise using the problematic notes and syllables, beginning one word before the problem note. Practice the exercise—then try it a half step higher and a then a half step lower. This kind of practice will help you recognize and correct problems quickly.

Explosive and Voiced Consonants

In singing, consonants set the vowels into motion and require more powerful articulation than in speech. The consonants "t," "p," and "k" are called *explosive consonants,* because they are produced with an explosion of air. "D," "b," and "g" are called *voiced consonants,* because they are the voiced counterparts of "t," "p," and "k," respectively. Let's look at the importance of these consonants to the singer.

If you do not explode air when pronouncing a "t," you will produce the consonant "d" instead. Check your songs for words that contain the consonant "t." Be sure to explode the "t" clearly when you sing those words which contain it. For example, recall the word "that" in "Bye, Bye Baby."

> Though you'll be gone for a while
> I know that I'll be smiling.

If you don't fully explode the "t," it becomes a "d" sound.

> I know thad I'll be smiling.

The consonant "t" also requires special attention in the song "Personality." The word "personality" is easily sung "personalidy."

Like "t," the letter "p" is an explosive consonant. Although Americans do not emphasize the "p" in speech, it must be pronounced clearly when sung. If the consonant "p" is not fully exploded, the consonant "b" will result.

Listen to how clearly Barbra Streisand explodes each "p" in her hit "People" from *Funny Girl* by Jule Styne. In the hands of a less experienced singer, the lyric "people who need people" can become "beeble who need beeble." This sounds like an exaggeration, but if you listen to other singers—you'll be amazed at how often this mistake occurs.

Take a look at the consonant "p," as used in "Solomon Song" from *The Threepenny Opera* (English words by Marc Blitzstein and music by Kurt Weill).

Then the poor dope
Went soft as soap

If the consonant "p" is not exploded clearly, a "b" sound results.

Then the poor dobe
Went soft as soab

The consonant "k" becomes "g" when not properly exploded. Consider this line from "Personality."

And think of all the books
About DuBarry's looks.

If not well-articulated, the "k" sounds like its voiced counterpart, "g."

And think of all the boogs
About Dubarry's loogs.

Sometimes the explosive consonant sound "k" is mispronounced as an "h" sound. Thus, in "Far, From the Home I Love" from *Fiddler on the Roof* by Bock and Harnick, the line "How can I hope to make you understand" becomes "How han I hope to make you understand."

Let's review the explosive consonants and the voiced consonants that occur when these are not clearly exploded. There are three explosive consonants which have voiced counterparts. Avoid substituting the voiced consonants for the corresponding explosive consonant wherever possible.

Explosive Consonant	**Voiced Consonant**
t	d
p	b
k	g

So far, you've learned how to handle the more difficult consonants—the nasal consonants (*l, m, n,* and *r*), vowel consonants (*y* and *w*)—as well as the explosive consonants (*t, p,* and *k*) and their voiced counterparts (*d, b,* and *g*). Now let's look at the remaining consonants.

Hissed and Sounded Consonants

"F," "s," and "sh" are sometimes called *hissed consonants* (although "sh" is not a consonant, it is a pure consonant sound). The consonant sounds "v," "z," and "dj" are the *sounded* counterparts to "f," "s," and "sh," respectively.

The consonant "f' is hissed when it is pronounced. If it is not articulated clearly, it becomes a "v" sound. Thus, in "Smoke Gets in Your Eyes" from *Roberta* by Jerome Kern and Otto Harbach, the line "So I chaffed them and I gaily laughed" can become "So I chavd them and I gaily lavd."

The consonants "s" and "z" do not usually pose problems to the singer. Be aware that a final "s" should often be pronounced as a "z" sound. For instance, consider these lines from "The Simple Joys of Maidenhood" from *Camelot* by Lerner and Loewe.

Where are the trivial joys?
Harmless, convivial joys?

If you don't sing a "z" sound at the end of "joys" an "s" sound results.

Where are the trivial joice?
Harmless, convivial joice?

The hissed sound "sh" (as in the word "show") should always be distinguished from its sounded counterpart, "dj" (as in the word "judge").

Consonant Exceptions

"C," "q," and "x" are not treated as individual consonant sounds in this section. The letter "c" is represented by other consonant sounds which have already been discussed: "k" (as in "can"), "s" (as in "cymbal"), or "sh" (as in "ancient").

The letter "q" is pronounced as a combination sound "kw" (as in "quick"). The letter "x" is pronounced as a "z" sound (as in "xylophone")—or as the consonant compound "ks" (as in "excellent").

Here is a chart illustrating the important relationships between consonants and how they are produced.

Consonant Chart

	Explosive	Explosive and Voiced	Hissed	Hissed and Sounded	Nasal
Through the lips or between the lower lip and upper teeth	P	B	F	V	M
Between the tip of the tongue and the upper teeth	T	D	S	Z	L/N
Between the back of the tongue and the soft palate	K	G	Sh	Dj	
Sides of tongue touching upper side teeth					R

The consonant "W" is produced with the vowel "oo"—sometimes called a vowel-consonant
The consonant "Y" is produced with the vowel "ee"—sometimes called a vowel-consonant
The consonant "H" is produced in the larynx and is classified as an aspirant

When you have difficulty with a consonant in a song or vocal exercise, refer back to this section, and check the "Consonant Chart" for the correct position of the lips, tongue, and teeth. You may find that sometimes a particular consonant is difficult because of the preceding vowel or consonant—so, be sure to include the word just prior to the difficult syllable in your practice exercises.

As an exercise, record yourself singing a song. Then play back the tape and listen carefully to your diction. Don't focus on tone quality or singing style, just listen to the pronunciation of the words to see if the consonants are clear and correct throughout.

Breathing

Breathing is something we do automatically—yet it is a very complex process. As you have learned, deep breathing oxygenates and purifies the blood—and it provides the essential support to good singing. As we go about our daily lives, we breathe naturally without thinking about it. The subconscious mind instructs the brain to lower the diaphragm when the air pressure inside the body becomes equal to the air pressure outside the body. It is essential to have more air pressure inside the body than is in the outside air. At a high altitude (where there is little air pressure), it is more difficult to increase the pressure inside the body. Athletes become well aware of this phenomenon when they participate in athletic games at high altitudes.

Diaphragmatic Breathing

As you have seen, the diaphragm is a dome-shaped muscular plate that separates the chest cavity from the abdominal cavity. When the diaphragm lowers, it acts like a piston in a vacuum, drawing air in automatically. As the air is used, the diaphragm rises and the pressure weakens until the process begins again. This deep breathing is called *diaphragmatic breathing.*

The diaphragm literally flattens the stomach when it lowers. If the stomach is empty, this process poses no problem. If it is full, the stomach must stick out to allow the diaphragm to move down. We have all experienced difficulty in breathing after overeating. When the stomach is already extended with food, the diaphragm can't work at optimum efficiency.

Normal breathing is *diaphragmatic breathing.* Watch a baby and you will see the abdomen move up and down as the diaphragm moves. If you lie on your back, relax, and breathe naturally—you will observe the same movement in your own abdomen. The trick is to duplicate this movement when standing. Stand, relax, and take a deep breath through your nose—allowing your abdomen and rib cage to move outward. You will see that you instantly fill with air from the bottom up, like a pitcher filling with water.

If you have difficulty breathing deeply, you probably have tension in your body that is interfering with your ability to relax—or you are closing your throat when trying to breathe. A proper, deep breath produces no sound. If you hear your breathing, you may be partially closing your throat. Panting will help you get the feeling of an open throat.

Intercostal Breathing

Intercostal breathing involves the expansion of the rib cage—in much the same way as a bellows expands. If you sit with your elbows on your knees and breathe slowly through your nose, you will feel your rib cage expand in this way.

A deep, diaphragmatic breath usually includes some intercostal breathing—although intercostal breathing can be done independently. Dancers learn to breathe intercostally, because they tuck in at the waist—and need to hold the abdominal muscles rigid.

Clavicular Breathing

Shallow breathing is also called *clavicular breathing*. The shoulders raise and lower as a small amount of air enters the upper lungs. This type of breathing is often observed in smokers—and it supplies little oxygen to purify the blood. Persons who are accustomed to clavicular breathing may sometimes hyperventilate during their first voice lessons. This is because they are not accustomed to taking the large quantity of oxygen provided by deep breathing. If this happens to you, simply sit with your head between your legs and you will quickly return to normal.

When you observe other singers perform, you may sometimes see them lift their shoulders as they take a very deep breath. This is because clavicular breathing is the last step in the process of taking a very deep breath—the diaphragm lowers, the rib cage expands, and the upper lungs fill with air. Most singing does not require this large a breath—but it does require a deep breath.

Breathing Technique

Both inhaling and exhaling are very important in singing. Inhaling air through the nose is probably the most efficient means of taking in air. The mucous membranes in the nose moisten the air—and this helps prevent the throat from becoming dry. When breathing through your mouth, you should take air in high against the roof of your mouth rather than straight in toward the back of your throat. Breathing directly in through your mouth can make your throat dry—which naturally interferes with good singing.

A quick breath through the nose, with the mouth closed, will form a vacuum—so it is recommended that you breathe through your nose with your mouth open. The opening can be very slight. This technique may take a little while to learn—but with some practice, it will become quite comfortable.

The most common error students make when breathing is to draw in the stomach after lowering the diaphragm. This forces air out of your lungs in the same way that you can force air out of a balloon by squeezing it with your hand. Instead, try not to draw in your stomach when the diaphragm is expanded. This will allow you to produce a steady flow of air in the same way that a balloon will naturally release a consistent stream of air until it is empty.

Singing requires a good supply of air in the lungs—and this must be used efficiently. The windpipe acts as a compression chamber to condense the air pressure as needed for volume or high notes. Drawing in the stomach also forces air against the windpipe and creates tension in the throat. As the air leaves the lungs, the diaphragm will gradually return to its domed position before lowering again.

A singer's breathing should be comfortable, easy, and relaxed. Each breath creates downward and outward expansion of the air—taken in through the nose with the mouth open. Professional singers know that deep breathing is the best way to produce a really beautiful sound. For some singers, learning to breathe correctly will improve their tone tremendously. For others, steps must be taken to eliminate interference with the free production of tone.

The controlled exhalation of air is regulated by the volume, pitch, and tone quality of the note sung. Other factors include the position and shape of the tongue, mouth, throat, and diaphragm—which all work to regulate the singer's vowel form and breath form.

Single Vowel Sounds

Learning to produce vowel sounds correctly will simplify the art of singing—and singing vowels in a certain, precise manner is perhaps the most valuable way to build your voice.

As a general rule, vocal exercises are based on the pure vowel sounds in the Italian language.

A =**ah** as in "art"
E =**eh** as in "ever"
I =**ee** as in "eat"
O =**oh** as in "owe"
U =**oo** as in "ooze"

In addition to the pure vowel sounds from the Italian, you will naturally encounter other single vowel sounds (derived from English) in vocal exercises and songs.

The vowel "a" may also be vocalized as "ay" (as in "ale"). However, be sure to sing it as a single vowel sound—"ay," not "ay-ee." The vowel "a" may also be pronounced "aw" (as in "law"). It is sometimes difficult for some singers to differentiate between this vowel sound and the "ah" in "art."

The English "ih" (as in "it") and "uh" (as in "under") are also single vowel sounds. It is difficult for some to clearly distinguish among "eh," "ih," and "uh." For instance, the word "pen" is commonly mispronounced "pin" (and this mistake is sometimes the effect of a regional dialect).

There are two other single vowel sounds that are found in many English words: "aa" (as in "ask") and "uu" (as in put). These two vowels are usually neglected in vocal exercises because they do not exist in Italian. So far, you have learned four pronunciations of the letter "a": "ah," "ay," "aw," and "aa." Notice that the two-letter system makes it easy to visualize the sounds.

One does not use all the subtle variations of the spoken language in vocal exercises. Variations of pronunciation are used in the performance of songs—and are usually guided by the ear of the vocalist. The study of speech will enhance a singer's ability to communicate in properly pronounced English when singing, as well as when speaking. In the same way, the study of singing will assist the speaker in producing sounds with beautiful, rich quality.

The single vowel sounds may be grouped according to their overall tone quality.

Vowel Sound	**Tone Quality**
oh, aw, uu, oo	Dark
ah, eh, aa, uh	Neutral
ee, ih, ay	Bright

Each vowel has a particular form. The bright vowels are produced with a wide position of the mouth and lips—and the dark vowels are formed by the depth of the larynx.

Each vowel also requires a specific adjustment of the lips, tongue, and palate. The basic tongue position for each vowel sound is indicated in the following chart. Notice that dark vowels are formed with the back of the tongue in a low position, while bright vowels require that the back of the tongue be in a high position. Neutral vowels are produced with a neutral tongue position.

General Vowel Positions

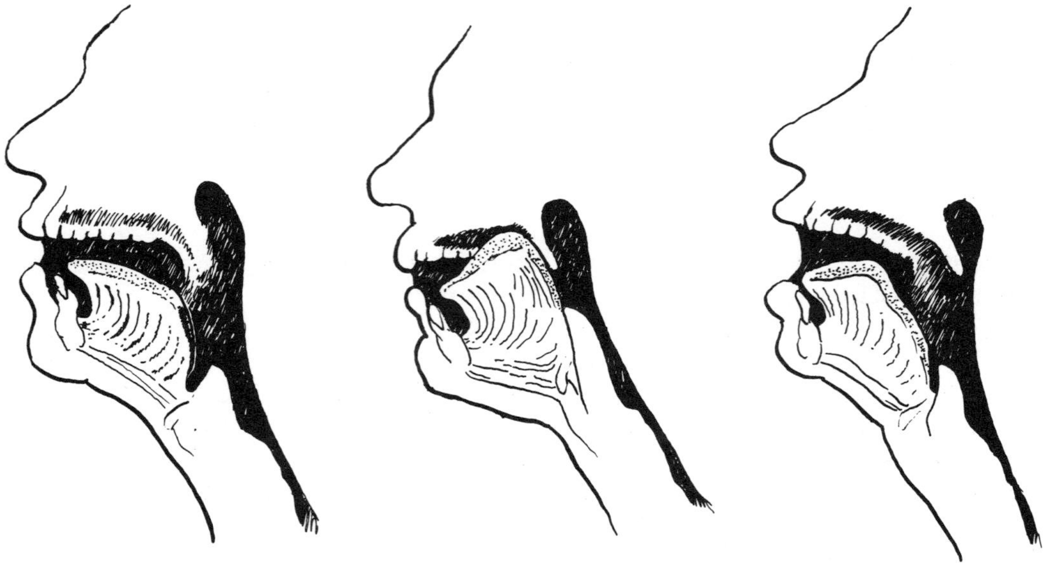

Dark Vowels
oh, aw, uu, oo

Bright Vowels
ee, ay, ih

Neutral Vowels
ah, eh, aa, uh

The shape of your face will make it easier to produce certain vowels. A person with a wide face will sing bright vowels with ease. A person with a narrow face will sing dark vowels with ease.

Be aware of the occurrence of single vowel sounds in any song you work on. It pays to devote practice time to singing vowels in vocal exercises. You'll be pleased when you see how this practice helps you produce beautiful, clear tones when you perform a song.

Double Vowel Sounds

As you know, vocal exercises are constructed to be sung on single vowel sounds—and often focus on the pure vowel sounds derived from the Italian language. The English language also features several double vowel sounds (technically termed *diphthongs*). These sounds are of particular concern to Americans singing in English.

In speech, a double vowel sound often seems like a single vowel because the two vowels are spoken together so quickly. In singing, a vowel is usually sustained—and double vowels become more obvious. For example, when spoken, the word "day" is pronounced with the consonant "d" followed by two quick vowel sounds—"deh-ee." When sung as a sustained note, the word "day" must be pronounced differently than when it is spoken. Imagine that the word "day" is the last word of a song, and must be held for three beats. In this case, the singer should sustain the tone on the first vowel sound ("eh") and then lightly add the second vowel sound ("ee") right as the tone is stopped at the end of the third beat. When used in this way, the "ee" sound is called a *vanish,* because it is so short and light that it seems to vanish away.

Here are three vowels which incorporate the short, light "ee" sound, or vanish, in a double vowel sound.

A =**EH (ee)** as in "ale"
I =**AH (ee)** as in "ice"
U =**(ee) OO** as in "used"

The "ee" sound also occurs in double vowel sounds formed with the vowel consonant "y." (Although the vowel consonants "y" and "w" are included in the section "Consonants," they are produced using vowel sounds—and are also included in this section.) Here are the double vowel sounds that occur when "y" is used.

y + ah = (ee) AH as in "yacht"
y + eh = (ee) EH as in "yet"
y + aa = (ee) AA as in "yak"
y + uh = (ee) UH as in "young"
y + ay = (ee) AY as in "yea"
y + ih = (ee) IH as in "yip"
y + ee = (ee) EE as in "ye"
y + aw = (ee) AW as in "yawn"
y + oh = (ee) OH as in "yoke"
y + oo = (ee) OO as in "you"

Some double vowel sounds incorporate an "oo" sound as a vanish. For example, the long "o" sound is pronounced using "oh" and "oo."

O = OH (oo) as in "no"

The "oo" sound also occurs in double vowel sounds formed with the vowel consonant "w."

w + ah = (oo) AH as in "wad"
w + eh = (oo) EH as in "wet"
w + aa = (oo) AA as in "wax"
w + uh = (oo) UH as in "was"
w + ay = (oo) AY as in "way"
w + ih = (oo) IH as in "wit"
w + ee = (oo) EE as in "we"
w + aw = (oo) AW as in "water"
w + oh = (oo) OH as in "woe"
w + oo = (oo) OO as in "woo"

So far, we have looked at individual vowels which are pronounced as double vowel sounds—as well as those double vowel sounds formed using the vowel consonants "y" and "w."

Some double vowel sounds are formed by putting two different individual vowels together.

OI =OH (ee) as in "oil"
OU =AH (oo) as in "out"

Note that these two sounds may also be spelled with a vowel followed by a vowel consonant.

OY =OH (ee) as in "boy"
OW =AH (oo) as in "cow"

It is very important that both vowel sounds are pronounced when singing double vowel sounds. Otherwise, the song lyric will be unclear. For example, if the "ee" vanish is omitted from the word "night," you get the word "not." Similarly, the word "light "becomes "lot" and "bright" becomes "brought." A regional error is sometimes heard when the double vowel "i" is sung before an "m" sound. An example is "toim" instead of "time" in Brooklynese.

There are many double vowel sounds in the English language. Determine where these sounds occur in all of your practice and performance material. Isolate any double vowel sound that seems difficult to sing and refer back to this section for help on pronouncing it correctly. Here are a few pointers on how to handle certain common situations relating to double vowel sounds.

- Be careful not to produce a double vowel sound when a single vowel sound is called for. For example, the word "shawl" should not be pronounced "sh-ee-awl," but "sh-awl."
- Complete a crescendo or diminuendo on the sustained vowel sound, not the vanish.
- When a word ends on a double vowel sound (as in "day," "go," or "sky") do not close your jaw on the vanish (though some pop singers use this technique as a special effect).

Since this is a book for singers of popular, rock, and Broadway music in English, there is naturally some departure from the standard singer's diction used in classical or operatic vocal study. Just remember, in popular music, articulating the words of a song is all-important.

You have learned many techniques and much information about singing. As you continue your study of voice, it is important that you continue to learn new songs. As your repertoire increases, you will also broaden your stylistic range and musical knowledge.

Glossary

Articulation. The action of the speech organs in the formation of consonants and vowels.

Bel canto. A style of singing developed in Italy during the Renaissance, characterized by brilliant vocal ornamentation and purity of tone.

Belting. A singing style used in pop, rock, and Broadway music, especially by female singers. Tones are produced in the middle and low registers of the voice using chest resonance which is amplified by diaphragmatic pressure.

Breath control. The ability to use breath conservatively and efficiently in order to sing long vocal phrases.

Breath support. Muscular support of the breathing process provided by the diaphragm and rib cage. Breath support creates a feeling of balance between the breath and the tone.

Bridge. The transitional section (or B section) of a song with AABA form. (Also called the **release**)

Chest register. The low range of the voice, produced using chest resonance.

Chord symbols. Abbreviations for chords, such as A7, C°7, or D♭m7.

Chromatic scale. A sequence of notes that progresses in consecutive half steps.

Clavicular breathing. Shallow breathing which occurs in the upper part of the lungs.

Connotative lyric. A song lyric that implies something more than the literal meaning of the words. (See **metaphor**)

Crescendo. A gradual increase in volume.

Diaphragmatic breathing. Deep breathing which involves the use of the diaphragm.

Diaphragm. A dome-shaped muscular plate that separates the chest cavity from the abdominal cavity.

Diminuendo. A gradual decrease in volume.

Diphthong. See **Double vowel sound.**

Double vowel sound. A complex sound composed of two vowel sounds.

Dynamics. Degrees of volume in a musical composition.

Eight. An individual song section, usually consisting of eight bars.

Embellishment. A note or group of notes added to a song melody—or to its rhythm, or harmony.

Enunciation. The pronunciation of words with regard to fullness and clearness.

Explosive consonants. The consonants "t," "p," and "k," which are produced using an explosion of air.

Falsetto. The high range of a male singer's voice, which resembles the normal range of a female singer's voice. (Also, the light, breathy head voice of the female singer.)

Form. The structure of a musical composition.

Grace note. An ornament printed in small type that borrows its rhythmic value from the preceding note.

G clef. See **treble clef.**

Half step. The distance between one note and the next adjacent note of the piano keyboard.

Head register. The high range of the voice, which is produced with head resonance.

Head resonance. The quality of tone produced in the high part of the voice when sung with normal volume.

Hissed consonants. The consonant sounds "f," "s," and "sh," which are produced with a hissing sound.

Hummed consonants. Consonants produced with nasal resonance.

Intercostal breathing. Breathing that involves the expansion and contraction of the rib cage.

Interpretation. An individual singer's stylistic treatment of a song.

Interval. The measurement of distance between two notes on a musical staff or keyboard.

Improvisation. A spontaneous interpretation of a song which may include changes in its melody, rhythm, or phrasing.

Key. The tonal center of a song or musical composition.

Key signature. Sharps or flats located at the beginning of the musical staff which indicate the key of the music.

Larynx. The body structure which contains the vocal cords. (Also called the *voice box.*)

Lead sheet. A chart containing the melody and lyrics of a song, with the harmony indicated in chord symbols.

Legato. A vocal technique that involves smooth and connected singing.

Legit. Short for *legitimate,* meaning the classical style of singing.

Lyrical phrase. A group of words that complete a thought or idea.

Lyrics. The words to a song—selected for their poetry and their ability to convey feelings of emotion.

Measure. A unit of musical time, usually composed of two, three, or four beats—the first of which is accented. (Also called a *bar.*)

Metaphor. A figure of speech in which one object is spoken of as if it were another.

Middle register. The range of the voice that is produced using a mixture of head and chest resonance. Also **middle voice.**

Middle voice. See **middle register.**

Mouth tones. The notes of the middle register that feel as though they are produced in the mouth.

Musical ear. The ability to recognize and differentiate sounds and pitches.

Musical phrase. A group of notes that form a satisfying feeling when played or sung.

Nasal or hummed consonants. The consonants "l," "m," "n," and "r," which are produced using nasal resonance (or humming).

Octave. A tone with either twice or half the frequency of a given tone—or the eight-note span between such notes.

Palate. The roof of the mouth, consisting of the hard palate and soft palate. The hard palate is the bony part of the roof of the mouth and the soft palate is the fleshy back part of the roof of the mouth.

Perfect pitch. The somewhat rare ability to sing a precise musical pitch without the aid of an instrument or tuning device. (Also called *absolute pitch.*)

Phrase. A natural division of the melodic or lyrical line, comparable to a sentence of speech.

Phrase mark. A curved line used to mark a musical phrase.

Pitch. The relative highness or lowness of a note, as measured in its vibrations per second. Also, a single musical note.

Pop. A genre of music characterized by contemporary lyrics, standard chord patterns, and electronic instrumentation.

Range. A span of notes; may be applied to a singer's voice or a piece of music.

Reinforced falsetto. The developed falsetto range of a male singer.

Release. See **bridge.**

Scale. A specific sequence of tones, beginning and ending on a key note (the note that names a key).

Sheet music. The printed version of a song—usually a piano/vocal arrangement.

Skip. Two notes separated by one or more scale tones.

Song form. The structure of a song, designated by letters naming each section, such as AABA.

Sounded consonants. The consonant sounds "v," "z," and "dj" (which are sounded counterparts of the hissed consonants, "f," "s," and "sh," respectively).

Staccato. Notes marked with a dot which are sung quickly and lightly.

Staff. The lines and spaces upon which musical notes are written.

Tempo. The relative speed of a song or song section.

Tessitura. The most comfortable part of a singer's vocal range.

Transpose. To change the key of a song.

Treble clef. Also called the **G clef.** This clef is most frequently assigned to the right-hand part of a piano arrangement.

Vanish. In phonetics, the faint, final part of certain double vowel sounds, such as the faint "ee" ending of the vowel sound in the word "sky" ("skah-ee").

Vocalize. To sing vocal exercises.

Voice category. A label designating voice type, such as soprano, alto, tenor, or bass.

Voice box. See **larynx.**

Voiced consonants. The consonants "d," "b," and "g" (which are the voiced counterparts of the explosive consonants "t," "p," and "k," respectively).

Vowel consonants. The consonants "y" and "w," which are pronounced as vowel sounds.

Song Arrangements

Here's That Rainy Day

Words by Johnny Burke
Music by James Van Heusen

Ebmaj7 Ab/C Gm/D Ebmaj7 Ab/Eb Ebmaj7 Abm7
day. Here's that
7
Db9 Bb7b5 Gbmaj7 Gb6 Gb+ Gb6
rain - y day they told me a - bout, and I
10
Fm7 Bb7 Bb7sus4 Bb°7 Bb7 Ebmaj7
laughed at the thought that it might turn out this way.
13

Bb9 sus4 Bb9 Eb Ebmaj7 Gb/Db Cm7b5
Where is that worn - out wish that
16
Cbmaj7 Cb6 Abm6 Bb7/Ab Bb7 sus4
I threw a - side. Af - ter it
19
Bb7 Db7/Ab Ebmaj7
brought my lov - er near?
22

Abmaj7 Ab7 Dm7b5/Ab Bb7/Ab Eb Cm7b5/Gb
Fun - ny how love be - comes a cold rain - y
25
F7 Bb7 sus4 Bb7 Bb7b9/Cb
day. Fun - ny that rain - y day is
28
Ebmaj7 Cbmaj7/Eb Ebmaj9
here.
31

Bye Bye Baby

Lyrics by Leo Robin
Music by Jule Styne

F9 F7 Bb D7 Gm Bb7
Al - though I know that you care, Won't you write
And just to show that I care, I will write
mf
8
Eb G7 Cm F7 Bb°7/Db
and de - clare That though on the loose,
and de - clare That I'm on the loose,
11
F7/C F9+ Bb B°7 Cm7 F7 Bb F9+
You are still on the square, I'll be
But I'll stay on the square, I'll be
p
14

Bb G+ G Cm G+ G Cm7 F7+
gloom - y, But send that rain bow to me
lone - ly, But ev - en though I'm lone - ly
18
Bb Bb°7 Bb Gm7 Am7 D7
Then my shad - ows will fly, Though you'll be
There'll be no oth - er guy, Though I'll be
21
Gm A°7/Gb Fm7 Bb7b5 Bb7 Eb Eb°7 Eb Cm Bb°7
gone for a - while I know that I'll be smil - ing
gone for a - while I know that I'll be smil - ing
mf
25

Bb Bb°7 Cm7 F7b9
1. Bb Em7b5 Ebm7b5 Dm7b5 Dbm7b5 Cm7b5 F7
With my ba-by bye and bye.
With my ba by bye and
dim.
29
2. Fm6/Ab G7 Abm6 B°7 Cm
bye, With my ba-by
f
33
F7 Bb Bbmaj7 Eb6 Bb
bye and bye.
p
37

Personality

Words by Johnny Burke
Music by James Van Heusen

Dm
Gm
C9 sus4 C7
F
cut - est per - son-al - i - ty." And think of
per-fect per - son-al - i - ty. A girl can
G9/B
Bbm6
all the books a - bout Du Bar - ry's looks What was it
get some - where in spite of string - y hair Or e - ven
F
Bb9
F
F#°7
C7/G
made her the toast of Par - ee?
just a bit bowed at the knee

C9 Bb°7 Dm Gm C9sus4 C7
She had a well de - vel - oped per - son - al - i - ty._
If she can show a fault - less per - son - al - i - ty._
F6 Cm Cm(maj7) Cm7
And what did Ro - me - o see in
And why are cer - tain girls of - fered
F6 Fmaj7+ F7 F7+ Bbmaj9 Bb7b9 Bb6 F7+ Bb Bb+ Bb6
Jul - i - et, Or Pi - er - rot in Pi - er - rette, Or
cer - tain things Like sab - le coats and wed - ding rings By

A7sus4 A7 Dm Gm7 C7
Jup - i - ter in Jun - o? You know!
men who wear their spats right? That's right!
Gm7 C7 G9/B
And when Sa - lo - me danced and had the
So, don't you say I'm smart and have the
B♭m6 F B♭9
boys en - tranced No doubt it must have been eas - y to see
kind est heart, Or what a won - der - ful sis - ter I'd be,

F F♯°7 C7/G C9 B♭°7 Dm
That she knew how to use her
Just tell me how you like my
Gm C9sus4 C7 1. F 2. F F6
per-son-al-i-ty. girl: A girl can
per-son-al-i-ty.

Scarborough Fair

Traditional
Arranged by Jerald B. Stone

Ab/Eb
Re - mem - ber me to
Eb/Bb Fm Eb Fm
one who lives there. She once
Eb Fm Eb Fm Eb Fm
was a true love of mine.

Fm7
mf
Fm
Eb
Cm7
Fm
Tell her to make me a cam - bric shirt,
Ab
Fm
Ab
Gm7
Bb
Pars - ley, sage, rose - mar - y, and

Fm
Eb6
Fm
thyme; With - out no seams nor
Bbm7 Fm Eb
Fm
Eb
Fm
nee - dle work, Then she'll be a
Eb Fm Eb Fm
true love of mine.
rall.

There Are Such Things

Words and music by Stanley Adams, Abel Baer and Geo. W. Meyer

Dmaj7
D7
Em7
are such things, Some - one to whis - per
G6
G♯°7
Dmaj7/A
F°7
"Dar - ling, you're my guid - ing star." not car - ing
Em7
A7sus4
A9
F9
E9
Em7
what you own but just what you are.

A7 A9sus4 A9 Dmaj9 D7+
reinforced falsetto
high falsetto
A peace - ful sky, there
G G6 A7 Em7
reinforced falsetto
are such things, A rain - bow high,
C♯7 F♯7sus4 F♯7 F♯7♭5/C B7 Em
high falsetto
reinforced falsetto
where heav - en sings, So have a lit - tle

G6 Gm6/B♭ D/A F♯m7 B13 A♯13 B13
reinforced falsetto
high falsetto
faith, and trust in what to - mor - row brings, You'll reach a
E13 Em7 A7 Em A7 D
reinforced falsetto
high falsetto
star be - cause there are such things.
rall.

Diamonds Are a Girl's Best Friend

Lyrics by Leo Robin
Music by Jule Styne

C G D7 G G°7/Bb D9/A D7b9
nen - tal But dia - monds are a girl's best friend,
law - yer, But dia - monds are a girl's best friend,
D7 E7 Am
A kiss may be grand but it won't pay the
There may come a time when a hard - boiled em-
E7 A Bm7 A°7/C A/C# Bm7 A7 D9 Am7
rent - al on your hum - ble flat, Or help you at the
ploy - er thinks you're aw - ful nice, But get that "ice" or

D9 D7 Dm G°7 G9 C B
au - to - mat. Men grow cold as girls grow
else no dice. He's your guy when stocks are
C Cm G B7 Em A7
old and we all lose our charms in the
high, but be ware when they start to de -
D7 G
end. But square - cut or pear - shape, these
scend. It's then that those lous - es go

Dm6/F
Bm7
E7
Am7
3
rocks won't lose their shape, Dia - monds are a
back to their spous - es, Dia - monds are a
D7♭9
1. G
2. G
C6
G
girl's best friend.
girl's best friend.